hook, stitch
& give

hook, stitch & give

30 creative crochet presents
by Kat Goldin

Kyle Books

To Mum, with love

First published in Great Britain in 2014 by
Kyle Books
an imprint of Kyle Cathie Limited
192–198 Vauxhall Bridge Road
London SW1V 1DX
general.enquiries@kylebooks.com
www.kylebooks.com

10 9 8 7 6 5 4 3 2 1

ISBN: 978 0 85783 216 0

A CIP catalogue record for this title is available
from the British Library

Editor: Vicky Orchard
Design: Louise Leffler
Photography: Kat Goldin
Styling: Nadine Tubbs
Production: Lisa Pinnell

Colour reproduction by Scanhouse
Printed in China on acid-free paper by C&C Offset
Printing Co., Ltd

contents

introduction

There is something special about giving a handmade gift. The birth of a baby, that memorable first day at school, holidays, birthdays or 'just because I was thinking about you' are all perfect occasions for making and giving.

My love of handmade presents arrived with the premature birth of my first son. Too small to fit into most other baby clothes, our prized possession was a small handmade hat from a friend. Looking back now, it was full of mistakes – she was just learning to crochet at the time – but he wore that hat daily until I could no longer pull it over his ears. It was as if he was carrying around a bit of love from his beloved godmother.

And therein, I think, lies the beauty of handmade gifts. It is not just about the finished object, but the love, care and thought that goes into the entire process – from picking out the yarn to sewing in the ends. It says to the recipient that they mean enough to us to give up our most precious resource for them – our time.

This book is filled with things to make for everyone in your life – from babies, to children, to friends, to men, to women and for all kinds of occasions. You may even find some things you would like to make for yourself.

Happy crocheting!
Kat
http://www.slugsontherefrigerator.com

getting started

yarns

Choosing yarn for gifts is really no different from choosing for yourself – think about how the recipient is going to use the item, how likely they will be to hand wash (or not) and buy the best you can afford.

Yarn has come a long way in recent years. An ever-expanding combination of weights and fibres is available with relative ease in your local wool shop or online yarn stores.

Acrylic

There is no doubt that acrylic is the cheapest fibre available. Inexpensive, with many of the newer varieties being soft to the touch and machine washable, acrylic is a good option for giving. However, bear in mind that acrylic yarns often don't wear well and they can result in pilled and misshapen items. They also have a tendency to 'squeak' against the hook.

Wool

You will see throughout the pages of this book that I show a strong preference for wool or wool blend yarns. Wool yarns, especially merino and Blue Faced Leicester, are a joy to work with. Most wool yarns available these days are soft enough to be worn against the skin. There are many machine washable wool yarns on the market – look for 'superwash' on the label, particularly if you are giving your gift to

someone who isn't a knitter or crocheter. It means your lovingly handmade present is more likely to be worn time and again by its recipient.

Other Fibres

The fibres that can be spun into yarn are seemingly endless. Cotton and bamboo are great for items that need a lot of washing. Linen and jute are good choices for homewares that need structure. If you have questions about how a yarn will behave, ask a member of staff at your local store for advice.

Substituting Yarn

In each pattern throughout the book, I have suggested a yarn that works well for the pattern in terms of weight, drape and washability. I have also given a few suggestions to help you find some alternatives. In each pattern, I have also included the amount of yarn required, the yarn's properties and the weight. To ensure you are successful in substituting yarn, choose one with similar properties.

The easiest way to substitute yarn is to look for yarn of a similar make-up. If the yarn called for is a 50/50 wool/alpaca mix, then start looking there. Of course you can substitute other materials, but if you are making something with a lot of drape, then make sure your yarn can do that for you.

Yarn Weight Conversion

Yarn comes in a variety of different weights or thicknesses.

UK weight	Australian/New Zealand weight
Lace	2 ply
Light fingering	3 ply
Fingering	4 ply
Fingering (4ply) Sport (5ply)	5 ply
DK (8ply)	8 ply
Worsted/Aran	10 ply
Chunky	12 ply
Super bulky/chunky	14 ply

hooks

Crochet hooks are predominately made out of wood, acrylic, aluminium or steel. Personally, I prefer the glide and feel of aluminium crochet hooks, as they are both affordable and work with most yarns. This is down to personal preference and it is worth trying out a few. I am guilty of only being able to use one particular brand of hooks for all of my crochet.

Crochet hooks are sized in relation to their diameter. A larger crochet hook will take more yarn into the stitch. Most of the time, larger hooks are used with heavier yarns and smaller hooks for finer weights.

Tunisian Hooks

Tunisian, or Afghan, hooks are the same as traditional crochet hooks, but with a longer shaft or flexible cord attached with a stopper at the end. Tunisian hooks for working in the round have a hook at both ends, although in this book, Tunisian will only be worked in rows. Tunisian hooks can be bought separately or as part of a kit.

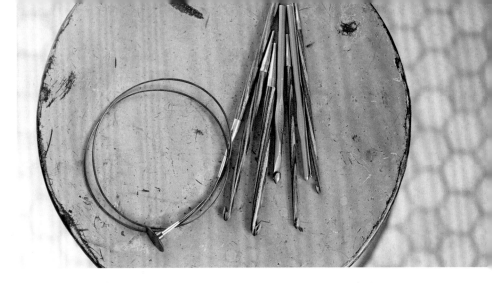

other supplies

Tapestry Needles

These have large eyes and blunt ends. They are used for sewing up or weaving in ends.

Stitch Markers

Use the type that have a split ring or are open, as you will need to move them with each round or row. I often use just a scrap of yarn or a safety pin as a stitch marker, rather than buying anything special.

Sewing Needles

Used particularly for sewing on buttons, these are thinner and sharper than tapestry needles. If you don't have co-ordinating thread for buttons, split your yarn lengthwise to thread through your sewing needle to sew on buttons.

Scissors

Sharp embroidery scissors are particularly useful for crochet, allowing you to make precision cuts, without a lot of bulk getting in the way or cutting your work.

Buttons

Possibly my favourite part of making a garment is choosing the buttons. Remember though, buttons can be choking hazards, so ensure that they are sewn on very tightly and are checked regularly.

sizing

For each pattern a sizing table indicates the key finished measurements. Each measurement has a guide for the age range the item will fit. Please remember that these are only guides. Where possible, use the actual measurements of the recipient to decide which size to make.

* Head Circumference: Measure around the head, just above the ears.
* Chest: Measure around the trunk, under the armpits.
* Bust: Measure the fullest part.
* Sleeve Length: Measure from the shoulder to the wrist.
* Length: Measure from the back of the neck to the waist.
* Waist: Measure around the natural waist.
* Hand Length: Measure from the wrist to the middle finger.
* Hand Width: Measure across the palm of the hand, just under the fingers.
* Foot Length: Measure from toe to heel.
* Foot Circumference: Measure around the ball of the foot.

Ease

The 'ease' of an item indicates how much bigger or smaller than the actual measurements the design is supposed to be worn. Items like hats are designed to be worn with negative ease (slightly smaller than head circumference) so they stay on. Jumpers and cardigans are generally sized with a bit of positive ease (bigger than the actual measurements) so they can be worn over other clothes. Underneath the sizing chart for each pattern is an indication of how much ease the garment is designed to have. If you are making for a baby that hasn't been born yet, think about when the baby is due to arrive and how old they might be when they need the item that you are making.

techniques and basic stitches

tension

Everyone crochets differently. Some people work very loosely, some more tightly. To ensure that your garments fit, you need to ensure you are working to the specified tension. For items such as scarves and home accessories, tension isn't that critical, as you will just end up with a bigger (or smaller) item. It is worth keeping in mind that tension that differs from the one specified will also change the amount of yarn you use.

At the most basic level, tension is the number of stitches and rows in a 10cm square. Each pattern in this book will give you the information as to how many stitches and how many rows it will take to make a 10cm square with your selected yarn and suggested hook size.

To see how your tension matches with the suggested one, make at least a 10cm square with the suggested hook size in the indicated stitch pattern. Then, if you plan to wash your finished item, wash and block (see Techniques, page 21) your swatch as you intend to wash your finished object. Let it dry completely and then measure your stitches and rows.

If you measure more stitches and rows in the swatch than the suggested tension, switch to a larger hook. If you measure fewer stitches and rows in the swatch than the suggested tension, switch to a smaller hook. Then, make another swatch and wash and block it, as you did the first, to double-check your tension.

holding your hook and yarn

Crochet hooks are sometimes held like a pencil, with your forefinger and thumb placed over the flattened portion of the hook, with the end of the hook coming out over your thumb. Others hold their hooks as you would a knife, with the end of the hook under your hand.

Hook held like a pencil

The yarn should be held in the opposite hand to the hook. It helps to thread the wool through your fingers to create a bit of tension and give you better control of your work.

It will take some time to find what is most comfortable for you. If you are just starting out, choose a project that uses a heavier weight yarn and larger hook, to make it easier to get to grips with the basic techniques.

Hook held like a knife

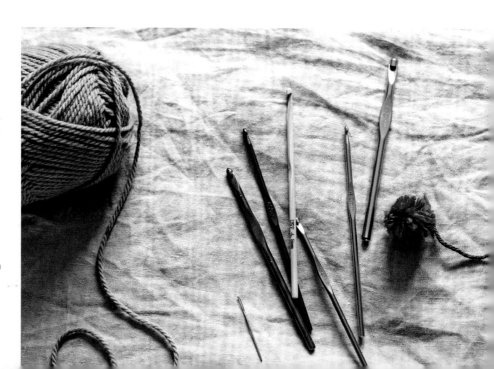

slip knot

Leaving a 10cm tail, make a loop with the cut end of the yarn behind the ball end of the yarn. Insert your hook into the loop, take the yarn over the hook and pull though. Pull on the tail end of the yarn to tighten the knot.

chain stitch (ch)

Begin with a slip knot on your hook and place your yarn over the hook. Twisting your hook slightly, draw your yarn through the loop on your hook. Repeat as many times as required.

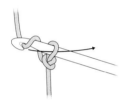 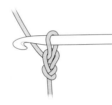

counting chain stitches

When counting how many stitches you have made, do not count the slip knot at the bottom of the chain or the loop on your hook.

turning chains (tch)

In order to get your new row or round up to the correct height, you will often be called on to make a turning chain. These are chain stitches at the beginning of each row or round. Usually, you count the turning chain as a stitch, except in the case of double crochet. However, each pattern will tell you whether the turning chains are counted or not.

Crochet stitches are different heights. Each stitch has a corresponding number of turning chains made at the beginning of the round/row:

1ch = Double crochet
2ch = Half treble crochet
3ch = Treble crochet
4ch = Triple treble crochet

Sometimes you will be called on to chain more than the number required for the stitch, in which case that will count as a stitch plus a number of chains.

anatomy of a crochet stitch

Post

The 'body' of the stitch. This is the portion of the stitch that is made of yarn overs. More yarn overs in a stitch mean a taller post.

Fork

This is the bottom portion of the stitch that connects it to the previous round or row.

Loops

At the top of the crochet stitch you will see two loops or a 'V' that is left after you have made the stitch. Unless otherwise stated, always work into both loops.

Bar

Half treble crochet stitches have a horizontal bar that runs at the back of the stitch. In some cases you will work into this instead of the normal Vs of the stitch.

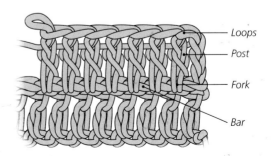

— Loops
— Post
— Fork
— Bar

slip stitch (slst)

Slip stitches are most often used for joining rounds or for moving the working yarn to a new point on the garment without having to add bulky stitches or break the yarn.

1. Insert the hook into the stitch.
2. Place the yarn over the hook.
3. Pull through both the stitch and the loop on the hook.

Moving yarn

Joining in the round

double crochet (dc)

1. Insert the hook into the stitch.
2. Place the yarn over the hook.
3. Pull through the stitch.
4. Yarn over the hook again.
5. Pull through the two loops on your hook.

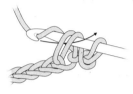

half treble crochet (htr)

1. Place the yarn over the hook.
2. Insert the hook into the stitch.
3. Place the yarn over the hook.
4. Pull through the stitch (three loops on hook).
5. Yarn over the hook again.
6. Pull through all three loops on your hook.

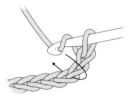

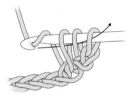

treble crochet (tr)

1. Place the yarn over the hook.
2. Insert the hook into the stitch.
3. Place the yarn over the hook.
4. Pull through the stitch (three loops on hook).
5. Yarn over the hook again.
6. Pull through two loops on your hook (two loops on hook).
7. Yarn over again.
8. Pull through the last two loops on the hook.

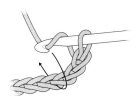

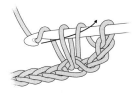

double treble crochet (dtr)

1. Place the yarn over the hook twice.
2. Insert the hook into the stitch.
3. Place the yarn over the hook.
4. Pull through the stitch (four loops on hook).
5. Yarn over the hook again.
6. Pull through two loops on the hook (three loops on hook).
7. Yarn over the hook again.
8. Pull through two loops on the hook (two loops on hook).
9. Yarn over again.
10. Pull through the last two loops on the hook.

raised stitches

Raised stitches are used in cable crochet and for making ribbing. They are made by working around the post/body of the stitch, instead of the top of the stitch. Raised stitches can be made with any of the basic stitches, but are most often used with treble crochet.

raised treble front (RtrF)

1. Place the yarn over the hook.

2. Insert the hook into the space between the stitch you are raising and the previous stitch, from the front of your work.

3. Bring the hook around the back of the stitch and through to the front of your work in between the stitch and the next stitch.

4. Yarn over hook.

5. Pull the loop back through the spaces between the stitches.

6. Yarn over and pull through two loops twice, as you would a normal treble crochet.

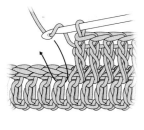
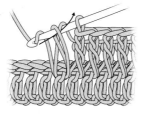
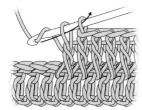
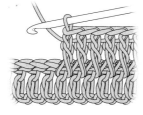

raised treble back (RtrB)

1. Place the yarn over the hook.

2. Bring the hook to the back of your work and insert the hook into the space between the stitch you are raising and the previous stitch, from the back of your work.

3. Bring the hook around the front of the stitch and through to the back of your work in between the stitch and the next stitch.

4. Yarn over hook.

5. Pull the loop back through the spaces between the stitches.

6. Yarn over and pull through two loops twice, as you would a normal treble crochet.

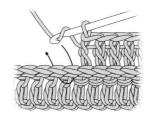
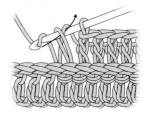
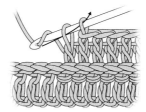
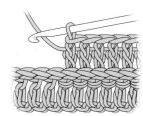

cabled crochet

Cables are achieved in crochet by crossing groups of raised stitches. It can be tricky to understand at first. In all of the cables worked in this book, you will miss a specified number of stitches, work a group of raised stitches, then go back and work the missed stitches so they cross over the front of the cable. You then continue working as normal in the pattern.

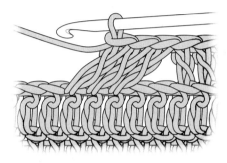

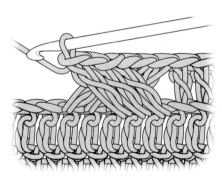

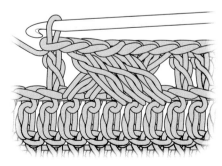

foundation double crochet (fdc)

Foundation crochet or chainless crochet is a way of working a starting row without having to work a chain. This is used in places where you need more stretch than a chain stitch can provide.

1. Starting with a slip knot, chain two.
2. Insert your hook back into the first chain.
3. Yarn over and pull through (two loops on hook). This links your stitches together.
4. Yarn over and pull through one loop on your hook (two loops on hook). This counts as your chain stitch.
5. Yarn over again and pull through the remaining two loops on your hook.

To continue:

1. Insert your hook into the chain stitch of the previous fdc.
2. Yarn over and pull through (two loops on hook). This counts as your joining stitch.
3. Yarn over and pull through one loop on your hook (two loops on hook). This counts as your chain stitch.
4. Yarn over again and pull through the remaining two loops on the hook.

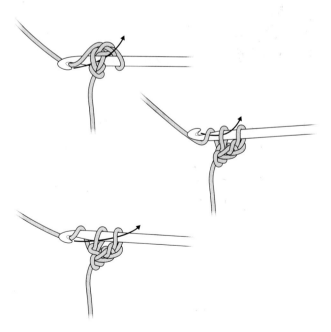

foundation treble crochet (ftc)

1. Starting with a slip knot, chain three.
2. Yarn over.
3. Insert the hook back into the first chain.
4. Yarn over and pull through chain (three loops on hook).
This links your stitches together.
5. Yarn over and pull through one loop on your hook (three loops on hook). This counts as your new chain stitch.
6. Yarn over and pull through two loops.
7. Yarn over again and pull through the remaining two loops on the hook.

To continue:

1. Yarn over.
2. Insert your hook into the chain stitch of the previous ftc.
3. Yarn over and pull through chain (three loops on hook).
This links your stitches together.
4. Yarn over and pull through one loop on your hook (three loops on hook). This counts as your new chain stitch.
5. Yarn over and pull through two loops.
6. Yarn over again and pull through the remaining two loops on your hook.

decreases

Decreases are made by working the specified stitch up to the last yarn over, then inserting the hook into the next stitch and working it up to the last yarn over. Then yarn over and pull through all the loops on your hook. This is often written in the pattern as 2tog.

double crochet two together (dc2tog)

1. Insert hook into the next stitch.
2. Yarn over and pull through.
Work steps 1 and 2 twice.
3. Yarn over and pull through all of the loops on your hook.
1 double crochet stitch decreased.

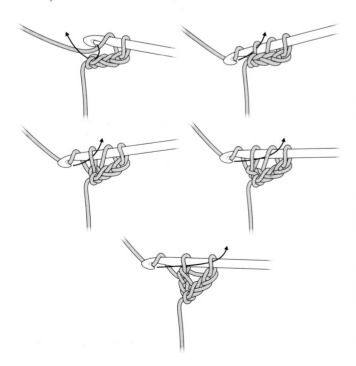

working in the round

One of the neatest ways to start working in rounds is with a magic loop (also called an adjustable loop). This is my preferred way of starting, as it enables you to get a very tight, closed first round.

1. Make a loop with the yarn, placing the cut end behind the ball end of the yarn.

2. Pinch the loop where the yarn crosses, holding the loop secure.

3. Insert your hook into the big loop.

4. Chain the specified number of stitches, using your magic loop as a slip stitch. This will help secure the loop.

5. Make the specified stitches, working around the loop.

6. Pull the tail end tightly to bring the bottom of the stitches into a circle.

7. After you have worked a few rounds of the pattern, tie off the tail end to prevent the magic loop from opening back up.

Tunisian crochet

Tunisian or Afghan crochet is a method that is worked with a crochet hook with a flexible cord attached to the end. Tunisian is worked in long rows, always with the right side facing. Each row has two distinct parts – the forward pass and the return pass. This book only uses two of the most basic Tunisian stitches and gives a great introduction to this incredibly versatile method of crochet.

set-up row (this is the same for all Tunisian stitches) forward pass:

1. Chain a length, starting with the second chain from the hook.

2. Insert the hook into the chain, yarn over and pull through.

Work step 2 until all chains have been worked. You will have as many loops on your hook as you have chain stitches, excluding the first chain you missed.

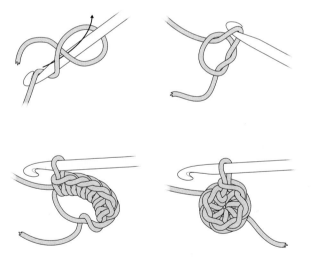

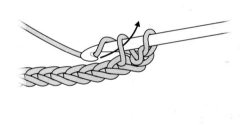

Alternatively, if you find the magic loop difficult, you can begin working in the round with four chains. Join with a slip stitch in the round and work your pattern into the loop created by the ring of chain stitches (not working into the individual chains, as you would when working flat).

standard return pass (srp)

1. Yarn over and pull through one loop on hook (this is the equivalent of your turning chain).

2. Yarn over and pull through two loops on the hook.

Work step 2 until only one loop remains on the hook.

Tunisian simple stitch (tss)

After working a set-up row and standard return pass:

1. Insert the hook into the next vertical bar created by the previous row.

2. Yarn over and pull through.

Work steps 1 and 2 to the end of the row.

3. Insert the hook into the chain at the end of the row, yarn over and pull through.

Work a standard return pass to close off your stitches.

Tunisian knit stitch (tks)

After working a set-up row and standard return pass:

1. Insert the hook from front to back, through your fabric, immediately to the right of the vertical bar created by the previous row.

2. Yarn over and pull through.

3. Work steps 1 and 2 to the end of the row.

4. Insert your hook into the chain at the end of the row, yarn over and pull through.

Work a standard return pass to close off your stitches.

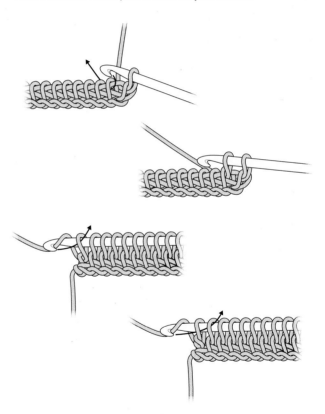

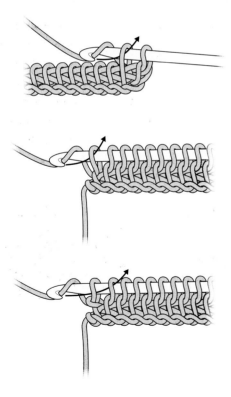

reading Tunisian patterns

Tunisian crochet patterns are read like other crochet patterns, but each row will give instructions for both the forward and return passes.

joining yarns

To join a new colour or ball of yarn seamlessly to your work, switch your yarn at the last yarn over of the stitch. For example, if I were switching when using double crochet, I would:

1. Insert the hook into the stitch.
2. Place the yarn over the hook.
3. Pull through the stitch.
4. Yarn over the hook again with the new colour/yarn.
5. Pull through the two loops on the hook.

You can easily work in any ends of yarn by working around them as you continue along the round/row. Simply lay them across the top of the row you are working on and continue crocheting into the stitches as normal.

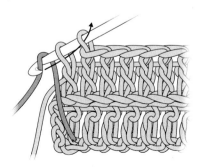

finishing

Once you reach the end of your work, cut the yarn, leaving at least a 15cm tail for weaving in. Pull the cut end through the last loop that remained on the hook to stop your stitches from unravelling. If there are yarn ends that you have not been able to work in as described above, use a tapestry needle to weave the remaining end securely into the back of your work. Weaving them into three or four stitches in three or four different directions will ensure they do not pop out later.

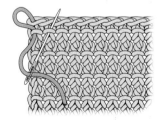 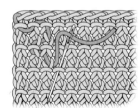

washing and blocking

Always use the ball band for your yarn as a guide to how to care for your finished item. Many will say 'Hand Wash Only'; however, if your machine has it, it is often OK to use a wool cycle on most handmade items. Test your swatch first. It's a good idea to include a note on the washing instructions along with your gift.

When working with yarns that have a high natural fibre content, you can block your project, which will help the yarn relax into the shape you have made. There are many different blocking techniques. Steam blocking uses an iron with a high steam setting. Press your work gently (not too hard or you will flatten the stitches).

Wet blocking can take longer to dry, but does tend to give most consistent results.

1. Wet your work in lukewarm water with a bit of wool wash in it.

2. Gently agitate your work.

3. Rinse your work in cool water and gently press the water out.

4. Place your work flat on a towel and roll it up to get more water out.

5. Lay the item out on a flat surface. Pin down the edges in shape using pins that won't rust.

6. Leave to dry fully.

sewing up

Slip Stitch Seams

Using a slip stitch to join different parts of an object creates a very strong seam. Line up the stitches of the two pieces you are joining and insert your hook through all four loops of the stitches on both pieces, yarn over hook, and pull the loop on your hook through the two pieces you are joining. Repeat to the end of the seam.

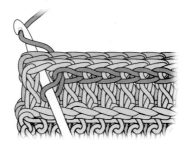

Running Stitch

Thread the needle with yarn and work up and down through the crochet fabric with even spaces between the stitches.

Backstitch

Backstitch is similar to running stitch, except you work some of the stitches back on themselves. Pull the stitch through the crochet fabric and then back into the underside behind where the thread came out. The needle is carried under the fabric to the far point of the new stitch, where it is brought up again and back to where the thread was brought up on the last stitch.

Whipstitch

Lining up your stitches, insert your threaded needle from the right side of the first stitch on the bottom piece and through the adjoining first stitch on the top piece from the wrong side. Bring your needle over the top of your work and back to the bottom piece, working into each stitch as above.

making a pom-pom

1. Cut a 30cm length of contrast yarn and set it aside.

2. Using the yarn still attached to the ball, secure the cut end of yarn between two fingers of your non-dominant hand and wrap it around them until it is at least 2cm thick (use more fingers for a big pom-pom and two for a small one).

3. Carefully remove the yarn from around your fingers.

4. Pick up the set-aside yarn and wrap it widthwise around the loops of yarn. Tie it off tightly.

5. Cut the loops, being careful not to cut the securing tie. Fluff up the yarn and trim into a pom-pom shape.

reading a pattern

Reading a pattern can be like reading a code. It can be tricky at first, but patterns are written using standard abbreviations for stitches and what to do. Know the code and you've got it!

Stitch or instruction	Abbreviation
Back Loop Only	BLO
Beginning Chain	Beg ch
Between	btwn
Chain	ch
Chain Space	chsp
Double Crochet	dc
Double Treble Crochet	dtr
Foundation Double Crochet	fdr
Foundation Treble Crochet	ftr
Half Treble Crochet	htr
Increase	inc
Place Marker	pm
Raised Back	RxxB (xx can be any stitch)
Raised Front	RxxF (xx can be any stitch)
Remove Marker	rm
Right Side	RS
Slip marker (move the marker up a row)	sm
Slipstitch	slst
Space	sp
Stitches	sts
Treble Crochet	tr
Treble/Triple Treble Crochet	ttr
Turning Chain	tch
Work 2 x Together	x2tog (xx can be any stitch)
Wrong Side	WS
Yarn Over	YO

Pattern Basics

Example: Rows 1–2 (3, 4, 5): 1 ch, [2dc in dc, 2dc] three times, 2 (3, 4, 5)dc, *2dc in dc; repeat from * to end. Join. Turn. 20 (21, 22, 23) sts.

✳ Numbers in round brackets ( ) relate to the instructions for the various sizes from smallest to largest, working left to right. They can be row or round numbers, stitch counts or repeats.

✳ The instruction '2dc in dc, 2dc' means make two double crochet in the next double crochet stitch, then double crochet in the next two stitches.

✳ Instructions in square brackets [ ] are to be repeated a set number of times, as directed immediately following the second bracket. There may be variations relating to the size, in which case follow the appropriate number in round brackets.

✳ When instructions are proceeded by a *, repeat that sequence of stitches as many times as indicated, usually to the end of the round or row.

✳ 'Join' means join the round.

✳ 'Turn' means turn your work.

✳ The stitch counts at the end of the row tell you how many stitches you should have worked in that row or round.

✳ 'Work Even' means continue in the stitch pattern as presented.

For the home

****

cabled throw

Thick and warm yarn, chunky cables – this large throw is deliciously soft and perfect for curling up under (even when you are making it).

skill level **intermediate**

Size	One size
Finished width	94cm
Finished length	150cm
Yarn amount	1632m

materials:

* 17 x 100g balls of Drops Andes (65 per cent wool, 35 per cent alpaca), Colour 0100
* 9mm hook

yarn review:

Fluffy like a cloud, this super chunky yarn makes a quick and gorgeous throw.

yarn alternatives:

Cascade Magnum

tension:

Work 9 sts and 11 rows in double crochet to measure 10cm square using 9mm hook, or size needed to achieve tension.

special stitches:

Baby Cable

Row 1: Miss next st, 1RdtrF one row below next st, 1RdtrF one row below missed st.

Row 2 and all WS rows: Dc across.

Repeat rows 1–2 as called for in the pattern.

Three Stitch Cable

Row 1: Miss next st, [1RdtrF one row below next st] twice, 1RdtrF one row below missed st.

Row 2 and all WS rows: Dc across.

Rows 3, 5 and 7: [1RdtrF one row below next stitch] three times.

Six Stitch Cable

Row 1: [1RdtrF one row below next st] six times.

Row 2 and all WS rows: Dc across.

Row 3: Rep row 1.

Row 5: Miss next 3 sts, [1RdtrF one row below next st] three times, 1RdtrF one row below each missed st.

Row 7: Rep row 1.

pattern note:

Do not count the turning chain as a stitch.

instructions:

Make 83ch.

Edging

Row 1: Starting in 4th ch from hook, 80tr. Turn. 80 sts.

Rows 2–3: 2ch, *1RtrF, 1RtrB; rep from * across. Turn.

Row 4: 1ch, 80dc. Turn.

Cable Pattern

Row 1: 1ch, [2dc, work row 1 of Baby Cable, 2dc, work row 1 of Three Stitch Cable, 2dc, work row 1 of Six Stitch Cable, 2dc, work row 1 of Three Stitch Cable, 2dc, work row 1 of Baby Cable] three times, 2dc. Turn.

Row 2 and all WS rows: 1ch, dc across.

Row 3: 1ch, [2dc, work row 1 of Baby Cable, 2dc, work row 3 of Three Stitch Cable, 2dc, work row 3 of Six Stitch Cable, 2dc, work row 3 of Three Stitch Cable, 2dc, work row 1 of Baby Cable] three times, 2dc. Turn.

Row 5: 1ch, [2dc, work row 1 of Baby Cable, 2dc, work row 5 of Three Stitch Cable, 2dc, work row 5 of Six Stitch Cable, 2dc work row 5 of Three Stitch Cable, 2dc, work row 5 of Baby Cable] three times, 2dc. Turn.

Row 7: 1ch, [2dc, work row 1 of Baby Cable, 2dc, work row 7 of Three Stitch Cable, 2dc, work row 7 of Six Stitch Cable, 2dc, work

row 7 of Three Stitch Cable, 2dc, work row 7 of Baby Cable] three times, 2dc. Turn.

Rows 9–120: Work rows 1–8 a further 14 times.

Edging

Row 1: 3ch, 80htr. Turn.

Rows 2–4: 3ch, *1RtrF, 1RtrB; rep from * across. Turn.

Finishing

Weave in the ends. Block to size.

For a different look, work the ribbing in a contrasting colour.

cabled cushion

Cloud-like alpaca wool blend yarn creates a squishy
cabled cushion – a perfect dream.

skill level **intermediate**

Size	One size
Finished width	40cm
Finished length	40cm
Yarn amount	367m

materials:

* 4 x 100g balls of Drops Andes (65 per
  cent wool, 35 per cent alpaca), Colour
  0100
* 9mm hook
* 40cm square cushion pad

yarn review:

This is the softest super chunky yarn I know
of – beautifully soft, it comes in a gorgeous
range of colours and is very affordable.

yarn alternative:

Cascade Magnum

tension:

Work 9 sts and 11 rows in double crochet
to measure 10cm sqaure using 9mm hook,
or size needed to achieve tension.

special stitches:

Baby Cable

Row 1: Miss next st, 1RdtrF one row below next st, 1RdtrF one row below missed st.
Row 2 and all WS rows: Dc across.
Repeat rows 1–2 as called for in the pattern.

Three Stitch Cable

Row 1: [1RdtrF one row below next st] three times.
Row 2 and all WS rows: Dc across.
Row 3: Miss next st, [1RdtrF one row below next st] twice, 1RdtrF one row below missed stitch.
Row 5: Rep row 1.

Six Stitch Cable

Row 1: [1RdtrF one row below next st] six times.
Row 2 and all WS rows: Dc across.
Row 3: Rep row 1.
Row 5: Miss next 3 sts, [1RdtrF one row below next st] three times, 1RdtrF one row below each missed st.
Work rows 1–6 a total of 11 times.

pattern note:

Do not count the turning chain as a stitch.

instructions:

Make 39ch.

Ribbing

Row 1: Starting in 4th ch from hook, 36tr. Turn. 36 sts.
Rows 2–4: 2ch, *1RtrF, 1RtrB; rep from * across. Turn.

Cable Pattern

Row 1: 1ch, 6dc, work row 1 of Baby Cable, 2dc, work row 1 of Three Stitch Cable, 2dc, work row 1 of Six Stitch Cable, 2dc, work row 1 of Three Stitch Cable, 2dc, work row 1 of Baby Cable, 6dc. Turn.
Row 2 and all WS rows: 1ch, dc across.
Row 3: 1ch, 6dc, work row 1 of Baby Cable, 2dc, work row 3 of Three Stitch Cable, 2dc, work row 3 of Six Stitch Cable, 2dc, work row 3 of Three Stitch Cable, 2dc, work row 1 of Baby Cable, 6dc. Turn.
Row 5: 1ch, 6dc, work row 1 of Baby Cable, 2dc, work row 5 of Three Stitch Cable, 2dc, work row 5 of Six Stitch Cable, 2dc, work row 5 of Three Stitch Cable, 2dc, work row 1 of Baby Cable, 6dc. Turn.
Row 7: 1ch, 6dc, work row 1 of Baby Cable, 2dc, work row 7 of Three Stitch Cable, 2dc, work row 7 of Six Stitch Cable, 2dc, work row 7 of Three Stitch Cable, 2dc, work row 1 of Baby Cable, 6dc. Turn.
Work rows 1–8 a total of seven times.

Ribbing

Row 1: 3ch, 36tr. Turn.
Rows 2–4: 3ch, *1RtrF, 1RtrB; rep from * across. Turn.

Finishing

With right sides facing, fold the cushion cover so that the short ends of the ribbing overlap by 10cm. Sew up the sides of the cushion cover. Turn right side out and insert the cushion pad.

This is a complementary cable pattern to the Cabled Throw, so make it in the same colour for a set.

kitschy koo pot holders

These retro-inspired, embroidered pot holders with their double layer are as practical as they are beautiful. And there's a choice of two designs.

skill level **beginner**

Size	One size
Finished size	18cm square
Yarn amount (Colour A)	110m
Yarn amount (Colour B)	20m
Yarn amount (Colour C)	20m

materials:

* Colour A: 1 x 50g ball of Rico Essentials Cotton DK (100 per cent cotton), Nature (51)
* Colour B: 1 x 50g ball of Rico Essentials Cotton DK (100 per cent cotton), Dusky Rose (51)
* Colour C: 1 x 50g ball of Rico Essentials Cotton DK (100 per cent cotton), Berry (51)
* 4mm hook

yarn review:

This mercerised DK weight cotton comes in a rainbow of colours.

yarn alternative:

James C Brett Cotton On

tension:

Work 19 sts and 20 rows in double crochet to measure 10cm square using 4mm hook, or size needed to achieve tension.

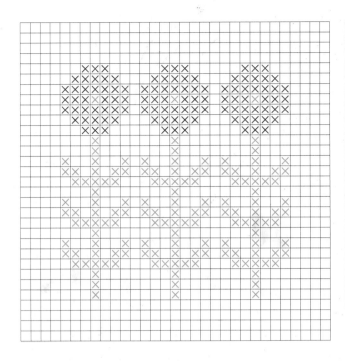

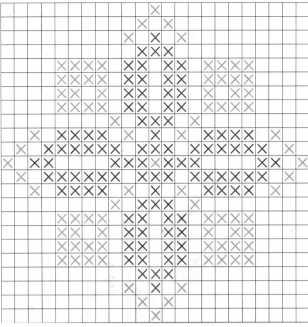

Blocking first opens out the stitches and makes the fabric much easier to embroider.

pattern (make 2 for each potholder)

In Colour A, 32ch.

Row 1: Starting in 2nd ch from hook, 31dc.

Rows 2–31: 1ch, 31dc.

embroidery

Wash and dry the squares. Using each stitch as a square on the chart, embroider one of the squares with your choice of design.

finishing

Place the embroidered square right side up on top of the plain square. With the embroidered square facing, attach Colour B at the top left-hand corner. Working through both layers, dc in each stitch and row around the square, working 3 sts into the stitch at the corners and slst to join.

Without turning, attach Colour C, 15ch, 1dc in the corner stitch, 1dc in each stitch around the square, 3dc in each corner stitch. When you reach the chain, work 1dc into each ch and slst to finish. Weave in ends.

linen snowflakes and stars

Tiny and delicate, these linen motifs make a beautiful addition to holiday décor. String them for a garland, use them in giftwrapping or put them on the Christmas tree.

skill level **beginner**

	Snowflake	Star
Finished width	9cm	9cm
Yarn amount	13m	10m

materials:

* 1 x 50g ball of 3-ply Linen Thread (100 per cent wetspun linen), White
* 1.25mm hook

yarn review:

This lace-weight linen thread holds its shape without blocking.

yarn alternative:

DMC Petra 3

tension:

1 motif measures 9cm wide.

special stitches:

Bobble Stitch (BS)

[YO, insert the hook into the stitch, YO and pull through the stitch, YO and pull through two loops] three times, YO and pull through all the loops on your hook.

Treble Picot (tr pic)

Make 5 chain, slip stitch into the first chain, [5 chain, slip stitch into the same chain as the 1st slip stitch] twice.

Picot (pic)

Make 5 chain, slip stitch into the first chain made.

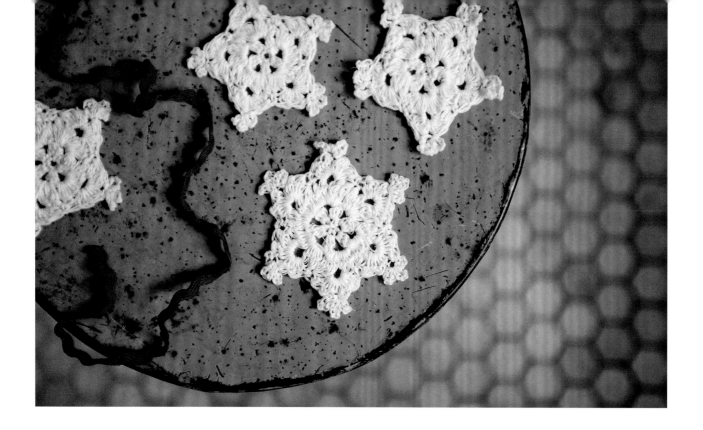

pattern notes:

Do not count the beginning chain as a stitch.
Work with the RS facing.

Linen thread can be tricky to work with, but its structure really helps these little flakes keep their shape.

snowflake instructions:

Round 1: Working into magic loop (see Techniques, page 17), 1ch, 6dc. Join.

Round 2: 3ch, [1BS, 2ch] six times. Join. 6 sts.

Round 3: 2slst to next chsp, [(2BS, 3ch, 2BS, 1ch) into next chsp, miss 1BS] six times. Join. 24 sts.

Round 4: 1ch, [miss 2BS, (2BS, 1tr pic, 2BS) into next chsp, miss 2BS, 1dc into 1chsp] six times. Join. 30 sts.

star instructions:

Round 1: Working into magic loop, 1ch, 5dc. Join.

Round 2: 3ch, [1BS, 2ch] five times. Join. 5 sts.

Round 3: 2slst to next chsp, [(3ch, 2BS, 3ch, 2BS, 1ch) into next chsp, miss 1BS], five times. Join. 20 sts.

Round 4: 1ch, [miss 2BS, (2BS, 1pic, 2BS) into next chsp, miss 2BS, 1dc into 1chsp] five times. 25 sts.

instructions:

Block lightly. For the best results, pin each of the picot points to let them dry into shape. To make bunting x 20ch, [1dc into the central picot point on one snowflake, 25ch]. Repeat for as many snowflakes as you have made.

christmas wreath

These wreaths are quick and addictive to make.

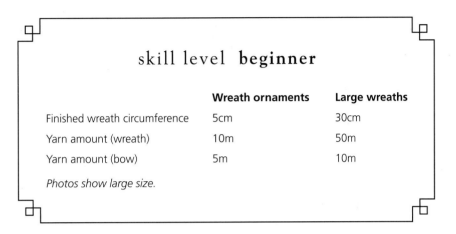

skill level **beginner**

	Wreath ornaments	Large wreaths
Finished wreath circumference	5cm	30cm
Yarn amount (wreath)	10m	50m
Yarn amount (bow)	5m	10m

Photos show large size.

materials:

For Wreath Ornament

* 1 x 50g ball of Rico Creative Cotton (100 per cent cotton), White (Wreath)
* 1 x 50g ball of Rico Creative Cotton (100 per cent cotton), Red (Bow)
* 1 x 3.5cm diameter curtain hoop per ornament
* 3.5mm hook

For Large Wreath

* 1 x 100g ball Texere Chunky Wool (100 per cent wool), White (Wreath)
* 1 x 100g ball Texere Chunky Wool (100 per cent wool), Red (Bow)
* 20cm embroidery hoop
* Small amount of ribbon for hanging
* 5.5mm hook

yarn review:

Both of the yarns for the wreath have excellent stitch definition and a good amount of structure to ensure the wreath is held open.

yarn alternative:

This pattern is easily adapted to use any yarn you may have to hand.

tension:

Gauge isn't crucial to this pattern, but use a small enough hook to achieve a tight tension.

pattern note:

If your tension or hoop size is different from the pattern, simply ensure you are using a multiple of three in round 1 and work the remaining rounds from there.

By no means limited to Christmas,
use different colours for every season.

instructions:

With yarn for the wreath, start with a slip knot on your hook. Insert the hook through the hoop just next to the screw fitting, YO and pull through the hoop and the loop on the hook to secure the yarn to the hoop.

Round 1: Working around the hoop, 51 (81) dc around. Join round by making slst into 1st dc of round, working in front of screw fitting.

Round 2: 1ch, *1dc, 3ch, miss 2; rep from * around. Do not join. 17 (27) chsp.

Round 3: 1dc into the 1st chsp, 4ch. *1dc into next chsp, 4ch; rep from * around. Do not join.

Round 4: 1dc into the 1st chsp, 5ch. *1dc into the next chsp, 5ch; rep from * around. Do not join.

Break yarn.

Bow

Using yarn for the bow, leaving a 4cm tail, 30ch. Join the chain into a loop.

Round 1: 1ch, 30dc. Do not join.

Work round 1 a total of six times.

Cut your yarn, leaving a 45cm tail.

Align the tails in the centre of the bow.

Use the long tail to wrap around the middle of the bow until you are left with a 7.5cm tail. Use the tails to secure the bow to the wreath.

Finishing

Block and pin the wreath to help it keep its shape. Spray starch may also help. Tie a piece of ribbon to the screw fitting for hanging.

pouf and it's gone

Hide extra duvets in this patterned pouf.
A removable seal means that you can take
the pouf apart for washing.

skill level **beginner**

Size	One size
Diameter	193cm
Yarn amount	240m

materials:

* 3 x 500g cones of Fireside Yarn T-shirt
  Yarn (100 per cent cotton jersey), Purple
  Passion
* 9mm hook
* 1 double duvet with cover (cover
  shows through the pouf, so pick
  complementary colours)

yarn review:

This super chunky-weight, T-shirt yarn comes
in every colour of the rainbow.

yarn alternative:

Hoopla T-shirt Yarn

tension:

Work 8 sts and 3 rows in treble crochet to
measure 10cm square using 9mm hook,
or size needed to achieve tension.

pattern notes:

Count the 3ch at the beginning of the round
as a stitch.
The pattern is worked without turning,
RS facing.

T-shirt yarn is a fantastic choice for homewares – it washes incredibly well and works up lightning fast, making big projects a dream.

instructions:

Round 1: Working into magic loop (see Techniques, page 17), 6ch (counts as 1tr and 3ch), [1tr, 3ch] six times. Join. 7 tr.

Round 2: 3ch, 1tr in same st, 3ch, [2tr in next tr, 3ch] six times. Join. 14 tr.

Round 3: 3ch, 1tr in same st, 1tr, 3ch, [2tr in next tr, 1tr, 3ch] six times. Join. 21 tr.

Round 4: 3ch, 1tr in same st, 1tr, 2tr in next tr, 3ch, [2tr in next tr, 1tr, 2tr in next tr, 3ch] six times. Join. 35 tr.

Round 5: 3ch, 1tr in same st, 3tr, 2tr in next tr, 3ch, [2tr in next tr, 3tr, 2tr in next tr, 3ch] six times. Join. 49 tr.

Round 6: 3ch, 1tr in same st, 2tr, 2tr in next tr, 3ch, [2tr in next tr, 2tr, 3ch, miss next tr, 2tr, 2tr in next tr, 3ch] six times. Join. 56 tr.

Round 7: 3ch, 1tr in same st, 2tr, 3ch, miss next tr, 1tr in 3chsp, 3ch, miss next tr, 2tr, 2tr in next tr, 3ch, [2tr in next tr, 2tr, 3ch, miss next tr, 1tr in 3chsp, 3ch, miss next tr, 2tr, 2tr in next tr, 3ch] six times. Join. 63 tr.

Round 8: 3ch, 1tr in same st, 2tr, 3ch, miss next tr, 1tr in chsp, 1tr in tr, 1tr in chsp, 3ch, miss next tr, 2tr, 2tr in next tr, 3ch, [2tr in next tr, 2tr, 3ch, miss next tr, 1tr in chsp, 1tr in tr, 1tr in chsp, 3ch, miss next tr, 2tr, 2tr in next tr, 3ch] six times. Join. 77 tr.

Round 9: 3ch, 1tr in same st, 2tr, 3ch, miss next tr and chsp, 2tr in next tr, 1tr, 2tr in next tr, miss next tr, 3ch, miss 3chsp and next tr, 2tr, 2tr in next tr, 3ch, [2tr in next tr, 2tr, 3ch, miss next tr and chsp, 2tr in next tr, 1tr, 2tr in next tr, miss next tr, 3ch, miss 3chsp and next tr, 2tr, 2tr in next tr, 3ch] six times. Join. 91 tr.

Round 10: 3ch, 1tr in same st, 2tr, 3ch, miss next tr and chsp, 2tr in next tr, 1tr, 3ch, miss next tr, 1tr, 2tr in next tr, miss next tr, 3ch, miss 3chsp and next tr, 2tr, 2tr in next tr, 3ch, [2tr in next tr, 2tr, 3ch, miss next tr and chsp, 2tr in next tr, 1tr, miss next tr, 3ch, 1tr, 2tr in next tr, miss next tr, 3ch, miss next chsp and tr, 2tr, 2tr in next tr, 3ch] six times. Join. 98 tr.

Round 11: 3ch, 3tr, 3ch, miss next chsp and tr, 2tr, 1tr into chsp, 2tr, 3ch, miss next tr and chsp, 4tr, 3ch [4tr, 3ch, miss chsp and next tr, 2tr, 1tr into chsp, 2tr, miss next tr and chsp,

3ch, 4tr, 3ch] six times. Join. 91 tr.

Round 12: 3ch, 3tr, 3ch, miss chsp and next tr, 3tr, 3ch, miss next tr and chsp, 4tr, 3ch [4tr, 3ch, miss next tr and chsp, 3tr, 3ch, miss next tr and chsp, 4tr, 3ch] six times. Join. 77 tr.

Round 13: 3ch, 3tr, 3ch, miss chsp and next tr, 1tr, miss next tr and chsp, 3ch, 4tr, 3ch [4tr, 3ch, miss next tr and chsp, 1tr, miss next tr and chsp, 3ch, 4tr, 3ch] six times. Join. 63 tr.

Round 14: 3ch, 3tr, 3ch, miss chsp and next tr, 4tr, 3ch [4tr, 3ch, miss next tr and chsp, 4tr, 3ch] six times. Join. 56 tr.

Round 15: 3ch, 1tr2tog, 1tr, 1tr in chsp, 2tr, 1tr2tog, 3ch, [1tr2tog, 2tr, 1tr in chsp, 2tr, 1tr2tog, 3ch] six times. Join. 49 tr.

Round 16: 3ch, 1tr2tog, 2tr, 1tr2tog, 3ch, [1tr2tog, 3tr, 1tr2tog, 3ch] six times. Join. 35 tr. Break yarn.

Seal

Round 1: Working into magic loop, 6ch (counts as 1tr and 3ch), [1tr, 3ch] six times. Join. 7 tr.

Round 2: 3ch, 1tr in same stitch, 3ch, [2tr in next tr, 3ch] six times. Join. 14 tr.

Round 3: 3ch, 2tr in next tr, 3ch, [1tr, 2tr in next tr, 3ch] six times. Join. 21 tr.

Round 4: 3ch, 1tr, 2tr in next tr, 3ch, [2tr, 2tr in next tr, 3ch] six times. Join. 28 tr.

Round 5: 3ch, 2tr, 2tr in next tr, 3ch, [3tr, 2tr in next tr, 3ch] six times. Join. 35 tr.

Round 6: 3ch, 3tr, 2tr in next tr, 3ch, [4tr, 2tr in next tr, 3ch] six times. Join. 42 tr. Break yarn and weave in the ends.

Finishing

Stuff the pouf with the duvet. Insert the seal inside the pouf to keep the duvet secured.

colour block baskets

These hard-wearing baskets make a great gift on their own
or as hampers for other things.

skill level **beginner**

Size	Small	Medium	Large	Extra large
Diameter	18cm	24cm	30cm	36cm
Height	18cm	24cm	30cm	36cm
Yarn amount (MC)	60m	100m	160m	230m
Yarn amount (CC)	90m	160m	250m	350m

Photos show small size.

materials:

* Main Colour (MC): 1 (1, 1, 1) spool of
  3-ply Nutscene Fillis Natural Jute Twine
  (100 per cent jute), Fillis
* Contrast Colour (CC): 1 (2, 2, 3) balls of
  3-ply Nutscene Heritage Range Colourful
  Jute Twine (100 per cent jute), Marine,
  Terracotta
* 5.5mm hook

yarn review:

This garden twine comes in every colour
imaginable and lends itself to home projects.

yarn alternative:

Any twine or cotton string will work, but a
change in tension may result in a change in
quantity needed.

tension:

Work 12 sts and 10 rows in double crochet
to measure 10cm square using 5.5mm hook,
or size needed to achieve tension.

pattern note:

Do not count the tch at the beginning of the
round as a stitch.

*Be careful when blocking the baskets as the dye
on some coloured twines can bleed.*

instructions:

Round 1: Working into a magic loop (see Techniques, page 17) and CC, 1ch, 8dc. Join. 8sts.

Round 2: 1ch, *2dc into next; rep from * around. Join. 16 sts.

Round 3: 1ch, *1dc, 2dc into next; rep from * around. Join. 24 sts.

Round 4: 1ch, *2dc, 2dc into next; rep from * around. Join. 32 sts.

Round 5: 1ch, *3dc, 2dc into next; rep from * around. Join. 40 sts.

Round 6: 1ch, *4dc, 2dc into next; rep from * around. Join. 48 sts.

Round 7: 1ch, *5dc, 2dc into next; rep from * around. Join. 56 sts.

Round 8: 1ch, *6dc, 2dc into next; rep from * around. Join. 64 sts.

Round 9: 1ch, *7dc, 2dc into next; rep from * around. Join. 72 sts.

For size Small, continue to Sides.

For sizes Medium, Large and Extra Large ONLY

Round 10: 1ch, *8dc, 2dc into next; rep from * around. Join. 80 sts.

Round 11: 1ch, *9dc, 2dc into next; rep from * around. Join. 88 sts.

Round 12: 1ch, *10dc, 2dc into next; rep from * around. Join. 96 sts.

For size Medium, continue to Sides.

For sizes Large and Extra Large ONLY

Round 13: 1ch, *11dc, 2dc into next; rep from * around. Join. 104 sts.

Round 14: 1ch, *12dc, 2dc into next; rep from * around. Join. 112 sts.

Round 15: 1ch, *13dc, 2dc into next; rep from * around. Join. 120 sts.

For size Large, continue to Sides.

For size Extra Large ONLY
Round 16: 1ch, *14dc, 2dc into next; rep from * around. Join. 128 sts.
Round 17: 1ch, *15dc, 2dc into next; rep from * around. Join. 136 sts.
Round 18: 1ch, *16dc, 2dc into next; rep from * around. Join. 144 sts.

Sides

Work 8 (11, 14, 17) rounds even in dc with CC, switch to MC and work 5 (8, 11, 14) rounds even in dc.

Handles

Round 1 (32, 40, 49): 1ch, 12 (18, 24, 30) dc, 12ch, miss next 12dc, 24 (36, 48, 60) dc, 12ch, miss next 12dc, 12 (18, 24, 30)dc. Join. 48 (72, 96, 120) sts.
Rounds 2–5 (32–35, 41–44, 50–53): 1ch, 72 (96, 120, 144)dc. Join.
Break yarn and weave in the ends.

Finishing

Blocking your basket into shape will help smooth out some of the unevenness that is common when working with a stiff fibre like jute. If required, spritz with water and use a flat object such as a plate or tin to shape the bottom and plastic shopping bags to shape the top. Do be aware that the coloured twines may bleed when wet.

a place to perch

Make unexpected guests feel like they have the best seat in the house with these lovely chair pads (even if they are sitting on a spare stool)!

skill level **beginner**

Size	Rectangular	Large
Finished width	39cm	44cm
Finished height	26cm	44cm
Yarn amount (Colour A)	20m	25m
Yarn amount (Colour B)	230m	330m
Yarn amount (Colour C)	35m	35m
Yarn amount (Colour D)	85m	45m

Photos show rectangular size.

materials:
* Colour A: 1 x 50g ball of Drops Paris Cotton (100 per cent cotton), Pistachio
* Colour B: 5 (7) x 50g ball of Drops Paris Cotton (100 per cent cotton), Off White
* Colour C: 1 x 50g ball of Drops Paris Cotton (100 per cent cotton), Light Purple
* Colour D: 1 x 50g ball of Drops Paris Cotton (100 per cent cotton), Light Ice Blue
* 4mm hook

yarn review:
This hard-wearing DK-weight cotton comes in an amazing range of colours so you can choose your own colour scheme.

yarn alternative:
Rico Design Essentials Cotton DK

tension:
1 small motif measures 13cm square.

special stitch:
Popcorn Stitch (PS)

Make 5 trebles into the next stitch, remove the hook from the loop and insert from front to back into the top of the first treble. Insert the hook into the loop that has been left and pull through the stitch. At the beginning of the round, the 3 chains count as the first treble.

pattern note:
Popcorn stitches may need to be turned out with your fingers if they aren't popping out towards the front. The large size is an expanded version of the smaller motifs that make up the rectangular pad.

The puffiness of these popcorn stitches makes a perfect chair pad.

rectangular chair pad instructions:

Small Granny Squares (Make 6)

Round 1: With Colour A and working into magic loop (see Techniques, page 17), 3ch, [1PS, 5ch] four times. Join. Break yarn. 4 sts.

Round 2: Join Colour B in 5chsp, 3ch, *(1PS, 5ch, 1PS) into 5chsp, 3ch, miss 1PS; rep from * around. Join. Break yarn. 8 PS.

Round 3: Join Colour C in 5chsp, 3ch, *(1PS, 5ch, 1PS) into 5chsp, 3ch, miss 1PS, 1PS in 3chsp, miss 1PS; rep from * around. Join. Break yarn. 12 PS.

Round 4: Join Colour B in 5chsp, 3ch, *(1PS, 5ch, 1PS) into 5chsp, 3ch, miss 1PS, [1PS in 3chsp, miss 1PS] twice; rep from * around. Join. Break yarn. 16 PS.

Round 5: Join Colour D in 5chsp, 3ch, *(1PS, 5ch, 1PS) into 5chsp, 3ch, miss 1PS, [1PS in 3chsp, miss 1PS] three times; rep from * around. Join. Break yarn. 20 PS.

Join the granny squares. Using Colour D, hold two squares RS together. Work 3dc into each chsp, working through both squares to join. Using the photographs as a guide, join the granny squares in two rows of three.

Back of Pad

Using Colour B, 77 (86)ch.

Row 1: Starting in 4th ch from hook (counts as 1tr), 74 (83)tr. Turn. 75 (84) sts.

Row 2: 3ch (counts as 1tr), 74 (83)tr. Turn.

Work row 2 until the piece is 26 (44)cm.

large chair pad instructions

Work rounds 1–5 of a small granny square as for the rectangular chair pad.

Round 6: Join Colour B in 5chsp, 3ch, *(1PS, 5ch, 1PS) into 5chsp, 3ch, miss 1PS, [1PS in 3chsp, miss 1PS] four times; rep from * around. Join. Break yarn. 24 PS.

Round 7: Join Colour A in 5chsp, 3ch, *(1PS, 5ch, 1PS) into 5chsp, 3ch, miss 1PS, [1PS in 3chsp, miss 1PS] five times; rep from * around. Join. Break yarn. 28 PS.

Round 8: Join Colour B in 5chsp, 3ch, *(1PS, 5ch, 1PS) into 5chsp, 3ch, miss 1PS, [1PS in 3chsp, miss 1PS] six times; rep from * around. Join. Break yarn. 32 PS.

Round 9: Join Colour C in 5chsp, 3ch, *(1PS, 5ch, 1PS) into 5chsp, 3ch, miss 1PS, [1PS in 3chsp, miss 1PS] seven times; rep from * around. Join. Break yarn. 36 PS.

Round 10: Join Colour B in 5chsp, 3ch, *(1PS, 5ch, 1PS) into 5chsp, 3ch, miss 1PS, [1PS in 3chsp, miss 1PS] eight times; rep from * around. Join. Break yarn. 40 PS.

Round 11: Join Colour D in 5chsp, 3ch, *(1PS, 5ch, 1PS) into 5chsp, 3ch, miss 1PS, [1PS in 3chsp, miss 1PS] nine times; rep from * around. Join. Break yarn. 44 PS.

Back of Pad

Work as for the rectangular chair pad.

Finishing both chair pads

Place top and bottom pieces WS together. With the top facing, join Colour D and dc around the edge working into the chsps on the top and the corresponding stitches or row ends on the bottom.

table runner

This elegant table runner is made out of gorgeous, flower-inspired motifs.

skill level **intermediate**

Size	One size
Width	39cm
Length	156cm
Yarn amount	660m

materials:

* 2 x 100g hanks of Fyberspates Shelia's Sock (75 per cent superwash merino, 25 per cent nylon), Oyster
* 3.75mm hook

yarn review:

This hand-dyed sock yarn adds subtle colour changes and is supremely washable, making this a very usable table runner.

yarn alternative:

Artesano Definition Sock

tension:

1 motif measures 13cm across using 3.75mm hook.

special stitches:

Bobble Stitch (BS)
[YO, insert the hook into the stitch, YO and pull through the stitch, YO and pull through two loops] three times, YO and pull through all the loops on your hook.

Beginning Bobble Stitch (beg BS)
[YO, insert the hook into the stitch, YO and pull through stitch, YO and pull through two loops] twice, YO and pull through all the loops on the hook.

Cluster Decrease (cl dec)
[YO, insert the hook into the BS, YO and pull through stitch, YO, pull through two loops] three times, YO, miss (1ch, 1tr, 1ch) and insert the hook into the top of the next BS, pull through stitch, YO, pull through two loops, [YO, insert the hook into the stitch, YO and pull through stitch, YO, pull through two loops] three times, YO, pull through all seven loops on the hook.

pattern note:

You can omit the joining around and sew your motifs together if preferred.

instructions (make 36):

Make 5ch and join into a loop with a slst.

Round 1: Ch3, (counts as 1tr in a BS), working into centre of loop, 1beg BS, [3ch, 1BS] five times, 3ch. Join into top of beg ch. [6BS].

Round 2: (Ch3, (counts as 1tr in a BS), 1beg BS, 1BS) into BS, [2ch, 1tr into chsp, 2ch, 2BS into BS] five times, 2ch, 1tr into chsp, 2ch. Join into top of beg ch. [12BS and 6 tr sts].

Round 3: 2slst to 2nd BS, (3ch, (counts as 1tr in a BS), 1beg BS, [3ch, miss 2ch, 1tr in tr, 3ch, miss 2ch, 1BS, 4ch, 1BS] five times, 3ch, miss 2ch, 1tr in tr, 3ch, miss 2ch, 1BS into slst at start of round, 4ch. Join.

Round 4: (3ch, (counts as 1tr in a BS), 1beg BS, [1ch, 1tr into tr, 1ch, 1BS into BS, 5ch, 1dc into chsp, 5ch, 1BS into BS] five times, 5ch, 1dc into chsp, 5ch, Join.

Round 5: 3ch (does not count as a st), [1cl dec, 7ch, 1dc into chsp, miss 1dc, 5ch, 1dc into chsp, 6ch] six times. Join.

Joining round

When joining adjacent motifs, work that section of Round 5 as follows with Motif A being the motif you are currently working on and Motif B the motif you are joining onto: [1cl dec, 3ch, 1dc into the adjacent 7 chsp of Motif B, 3ch, 1dc into chsp of Motif A, miss 1dc, 2ch, 1dc into 5 chsp of Motif B, 2dc, 1dc into next chsp of Motif A, 3ch, 1dc into adjacent 7 chsp of Motif B, 3ch] repeat as required around otif A to join adjacent motifs.

Follow the diagram for the motif layout.

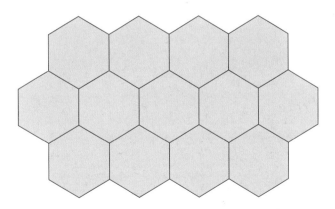

This would make a gorgeous host gift, paired with a bottle of wine or a bouquet of wild flowers.

zigzag hottie

This classic blanket pattern is transformed into a snuggly cover for a hot water bottle.

skill level **beginner**

Size	1-litre hottie	2-litre hottie
Circumference	33cm	43cm
Length	21cm	27cm
Yarn amount (Colours A and B)	40m	50m
Yarn amount (Colour C)	20m	20m

Photos show 2-litre hot water bottle.

materials:

* Colour A: 1 (1) x ball of King Cole Merino Blend Chunky (100 per cent wool), Saxe
* Colour B: 1 (1) x ball of King Cole Merino Blend Chunky (100 per cent wool), White
* Colour C: 1 (1) x ball of King Cole Merino Blend Chunky (100 per cent wool), Scarlet
* 6mm hook
* Safety pins
* 1-litre (2-litre) hot water bottle

yarn review:

This 100 per cent merino superwash chunky wool is gorgeously soft and very washable, making it perfect for a hot water bottle cover.

yarn alternative:

Wendy Merino Chunky

tension:

Work 10 sts and 10 rows in double crochet in BLO to measure 10cm square using 6mm hook, or size needed to achieve tension.

pattern notes:

Carry the yarn up the side of your work as you change colours to minimise the number of ends you have to weave in.
Do not count the tch as a stitch.

Made with chunky wool, this is the perfect last-minute 'Get Well Soon' gift.

instructions:

With Colour A, 40 (53)ch.

Row 1 (WS): Starting in 2nd ch from hook, 1dc, miss 1, 4dc, *3dc in next, 5dc, miss 2, 5dc; rep from * until 7 sts from end, 3dc in next, 4dc, miss 1, 1dc. Turn. 39 (52) sts.

Rows 2–4 (working in BLO): 1ch, 1dc, miss 1, 4dc, *3dc in next, 5dc, miss 2, 5dc; rep from * until 7 sts from end, 3dc in next, 4dc, miss 1, 1dc. Turn.

Rows 5–8 (working in BLO): With Colour B, 1ch, 1dc, miss 1, 4dc, *3dc in next, 5dc, miss 2, 5dc; rep from * until 7 sts from end, 3dc in next, 4dc, miss 1, 1dc. Turn.

Rows 9–12 (working in BLO): With Colour A, 1ch, 1dc, miss 1, 4dc, *3dc in next, 5dc, miss 2, 5dc; rep from * until 7 sts from end, 3dc in next, 4dc, miss 1, 1dc. Turn.

Work rows 5–12 a total of 5 (6) times. For the large hottie, work rows 5–8 once more.

Edging Row

Switch to Colour C, repeat row 2.

Sewing Up Bottom Cover

With WS facing, fold the cover so that the edging row will run vertically up the centre of the hot water bottle, with the ends overlapping by approximately 3.5cm. Pin in place. Turn the cover inside out and, working into the row ends, slst one end closed. Slst both ends of what will be the neck edge of the cover when closed, leaving a 7cm gap in the middle.

Neck Ribbing

Rejoin Colour C at the neck edge of the cover, 21ch.

Row 1: Starting in 2nd ch from hook, 20dc. 1slst into next 3 sts on neck edge of cover. Turn. 20 sts.

Row 2: 20dc in BLO. Turn.

Row 3: 1ch, 20dc in BLO, 1slst into next 3 sts on neck edge of cover. Turn.

Repeat rows 2–3 until all stitches around the neck of the cover are worked. When working into the overlapped section at the front of the cover, work through both layers of the cover.

Break yarn and weave in ends.

For Her

****

best bib and tucker necklace

Worked in a small amount of luxury yarn with delicate pearls, this vintage-feel necklace is quick and easy to work up.

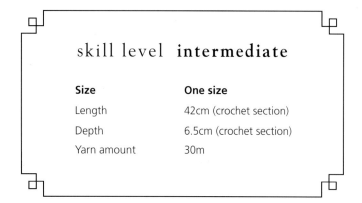

skill level **intermediate**

Size	One size
Length	42cm (crochet section)
Depth	6.5cm (crochet section)
Yarn amount	30m

materials:

* 1 x 50g cone of Jaipur Fino Silk (100 per cent mulberry silk), Cream
* 2mm hook
* 3 seed pearls
* Length of thread (for loading pearls onto the yarn)
* A chain bracelet with clasps attached
* Pliers, strong scissors or tin snips

yarn review:

This 100 per cent silk lace-weight yarn is simply glamorous.

yarn alternative:

DMC Petra Cotton Perle No 3 Crochet Cotton

tension:

The work measures 42cm x 1cm at the end of row 2.

pattern note:

Unless otherwise stated do not work into stitches, work only into chains.

instructions:

Make 147ch.

Row 1: Starting in 2nd ch from hook, 1dc, *4ch, miss 4, 1dc; rep from * to end. 30 dc.

Row 2 (RS): 1ch, [(2dc, 2htr, 2dc) in 4chsp] eight times, [(2dc, 1htr, 4ch, 1htr, 2dc) in 4chsp] 13 times, [(2dc, 2htr, 2dc) in 4chsp] eight times, 1dc in tch, rotate to work into other side (fch), [6dc into 4chsp] 29 times, slst into dc. Break yarn. 349 sts.

Row 3: Load pearls onto yarn for later use, with RS facing reattach yarn to 1st 4chsp created in row 2, (3ch (counts as 1tr), 4tr, 2ch, 5tr) into 4chsp [(5tr, 2ch, 5tr) into next 4chsp] 12 times. Turn. 130 sts.

Row 4 (WS): Slst to 2chsp, 1dc in chsp, [(3dtr, 1ch, 3dtr, 1ch, 3dtr) in next chsp, 1dc in next chsp] six times. Turn. 61 sts.

Row 5: Slst to chsp, 1dc in chsp, 5ch, 3tr in next chsp, 1ch, [(3tr, 1ch, 3tr, 1ch) in next chsp] eight times, 3tr in next chsp, 5ch, 1dc in next chsp. Turn. 56 sts.

Row 6: 3dc in chsp, 5ch, [miss 1chsp, 3tr in next chsp, 1ch, 5dtr in next chsp, 1ch, 3tr in next chsp, 1ch] four times, 4ch, 1dc in next chsp. Turn. 48 sts.

Row 7: 3dc in chsp, 5tr in next chsp, 2ch, [9tr in next chsp, 1dc in next chsp, 9tr in next ch sp, 2ch] three times, 2ch, 5tr in next chsp, 1dc in next chsp. Turn. 71 sts.

Row 8: Slst to chsp, [2dc in chsp, 6ch, 1dtr in dc, place bead next to hook, 1ch to secure bead in place, 1dtr in same dc, 6ch] three times, 2dc in next chsp. Break yarn and fasten off. 14 sts.

Finishing

Wet block to open out the lace pattern. Weave in the ends. Use the tin snips, pliers or scissors to remove a link from the centre of the bracelet. Sew the bracelet halves securely to the ends of row 2.

Combining different threads and beads will change the look and feel of this gorgeous gift.

shell scape

Normally, I'm not a fan of projects that are made in lots of parts (all those ends!), but this gorgeous shawl is worth the extra effort.

skill level **intermediate**

Size	One size
Finished wingspan	108cm
Finished depth from neck to hem	50cm
Yarn amount	610m

materials:

* 3 x 100g hanks of Ripples Craft Merino Sport (100 per cent superwash merino), Assynt Lochs
* 6mm hook

yarn review:

I can't say enough good things about this gorgeous, sport-weight superwash wool. It crochets up like a dream, with excellent stitch definition and drape.

yarn alternatives:

Cascade 220 Superwash Sport
MillaMia Naturally Soft Merino

tension:

1 shell motif measures 10cm high x 12cm wide at the base using 6mm hook or size required to obtain tension.

special stitches:

Puff Stitch (PS)

[YO, insert the hook into the stitch and draw up a loop] five times (11 loops on the hook). YO and pull through all loops on the hook.

Double Crochet 3 Together (dc3tog)

[Insert the hook into the next stitch, YO and draw up a loop] three times (4 loops on the hook). YO and pull through all loops on the hook.

pattern notes:

Motifs are joined as you go. Making each motif requires breaking the yarn at the top point. To minimise having to weave in ends, make sure to crochet over the loose ends (see Techniques, page 18).

When working the joining dcs up the row ends of the previous motif, exact placement of the stitches isn't crucial. Simply ensure they are evenly spaced up the row ends.

Do not count tch as a stitch unless specified.

instructions:

Basic Motif

Make 21fdc. Turn.

Row 1 (WS): 1ch, [1dc, 1ch, miss 1fdc] ten times, 1dc. Turn. 11 sts.

Row 2: 1ch, 1dc, [1ch, 1PS in chsp, miss 1dc] ten times, 1dc. Turn. 12 sts.

Row 3: 1ch, 1dc, [miss 1PS, 1dc in chsp] nine times, miss 1PS and 1ch, 1dc. Turn. 11 sts.

Row 4: 4ch (counts as 1tr and 1ch), miss 1dc, [1tr, 1ch, miss 1dc] four times, 1tr. Turn. 6 sts.

Row 5: 1ch, [1dc in tr, 1ch, miss 1tr] five times, 1dc in tch. Turn. 6 sts.

Row 6: 1ch, 1dc in dc, [1PS in chsp, 1ch, miss 1dc] five times, 1dc. Turn. 7 sts.

Row 7: 1ch, miss 1dc and 1PS [1dc in chsp, miss 1PS] five times, 1dc. Turn. 6 sts.

Row 8: 1ch, 1dc2tog, 1dc, 1dc2tog Turn. 3sts.

Row 9: 1ch, 3dc. Turn.

Row 10: 1ch, 1dc3tog. Fasten off and break yarn.

Motif Right Edge (MR)

Set-up row: Make 11fdc, RS facing, working evenly into row ends of previous motif 10dc from bottom edge to tip. Turn. 21sts.

Work rows 1–10 of the basic motif pattern.

Middle Motif (MM)

Set-up row: Join yarn to tip of motif, 10dc from tip of motif down to bottom edge, 11dc on next motif from bottom edge up to tip. Turn. 21sts.

Work rows 1–10 of the basic motif pattern.

Made in white or cream, this would make a beautiful wedding shawl.

Motif Left Edge (ML)

Set-up row: Working evenly into row ends of previous motif, 10dc from tip of motif down to bottom edge, 2ch (this forms the basis of the 1st fdc) 11fdc. Turn. 21 sts. Work rows 1–10 of the basic motif pattern.

Half Motif Right (HMR)

Set-up row: Make 11fdc, RS facing, working evenly into row ends of previous motif 10dc from bottom edge to tip. Turn. 21sts.

Row 1 (WS): 1ch, [1dc, 1ch, miss 1fdc] ten times, 1dc. Turn. 11 sts.

Row 2: 1ch, 1dc, [1ch, 1PS in chsp, miss 1dc] ten times, 1dc. Turn. 12 sts.

Row 3: 1ch, 1dc, [miss 1PS, 1dc in chsp] nine times, miss 1PS and 1ch, 1dc. Turn. 11 sts.

Row 4: 1ch, 5dc2tog, 1dc. Turn. 6sts.

Row 5: 1ch, 3dc2tog. Break yarn. 3sts.

Half Motif Middle (HMM)

Set-up row: Join yarn to tip of motif, 10dc from tip of motif down to bottom edge, 11dc on next motif from bottom edge up to tip. Turn. 21 sts.

Row 1 (WS): 1ch, [1dc, 1ch, miss 1fdc] ten times, 1dc. Turn. 11 sts.

Row 2: 1ch, 1dc, [1ch, 1PS in chsp, miss 1dc] ten times, 1dc. Turn. 12 sts.

Row 3: 1ch, 1dc, [miss 1PS, 1dc in chsp] nine times, miss 1PS and 1ch, 1dc. Turn. 11 sts.

Row 4: 1ch, 5dc2tog, 1dc. Turn. 6sts.

Row 5: 1ch, 3dc2tog. Break yarn. 3sts.

Half Motif Left (HML)

Set-up row: Working evenly into row ends of previous motif, 10dc from tip of motif down to bottom edge, 2ch (this forms basis of 1st fdc) 11fdc. Turn. 21 sts.

Row 1 (WS): 1ch, [1dc, 1ch, miss 1fdc] ten times, 1dc. Turn. 11 sts.

Row 2: 1ch, 1dc, [1ch, 1PS in chsp, miss 1dc] ten times, 1dc. Turn. 12 sts.

Row 3: 1ch, 1dc, [miss 1PS, 1dc in chsp] nine times, miss 1PS and 1ch, 1dc. Turn. 11 sts.

Row 4: 1ch, 5dc2tog, 1dc. Turn. 6sts.

Row 5: 1ch, 3dc2tog. Break yarn. 3sts.

Construction

See the schematic for visual instructions on construction.

Row 1: Make 1 Basic Motif.

Row 2: 1MR, 1ML.

Row 3: 1MR, 1MM, 1ML.

Row 4: 1MR, 2MM, 1ML.

Row 5: 1MR, 3MM, 1ML.

Row 6: 1MR, 4MM, 1ML.

Row 7: 1MR, 5MM, 1ML.

Row 8: 1MR, 6MM, 1ML.

Row 9: 1HMR, 7HMM, 1HML.

Edging

Rejoin the yarn on top of the straight edge, RS facing. Dc evenly across. Break yarn.

Finishing

Weave in and trim any remaining ends. Block to the finished measurements.

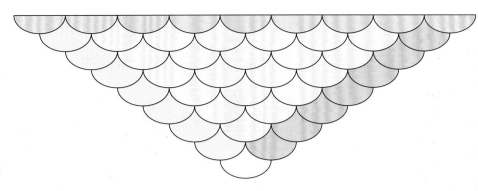

Motif Right Edge (MR)

Motif Left Edge (ML)

Middle Motif (MM)

Half Motif Right/Half Motif Middle/Half Motif Left

slouch and bobble hat

This is the perfect hat for hitting the slopes or the shops.

skill level advanced beginner

Size	Small	Medium	Large
Brim circumference	52cm	54cm	57cm
Height	26cm	27cm	28cm
Yarn amount (MC)	140m	145m	170m
Yarn amount (CC)	110m	115m	120m

materials:

* Main Colour (MC): 1 x 100g hank of Quince and Co Osprey (100 per cent wool), Bird's Egg
* Contrast Colour (CC): 1 x 100g hank of Quince and Co Osprey (100 per cent wool), Honey
* 5mm hook

yarn review:

This worsted-weight yarn has a smooth handle and comes in a rainbow of colours.

yarn alternative:

Cascade 220

tension:

Work 14 sts and 4.5 rows in Raised Treble Ribbing to measure 10cm square using 5mm hook, or size needed to achieve tension.

pattern notes:

Do not count the tch as a stitch unless stated.

This is a fun pattern to play with colour. Try keeping the ribbing and trebles the same colour and alternating colour on the double crochet stitches for a different look.

instructions:

Raised Treble Ribbing

With MC, leaving a 15cm tail for sewing up the gap in the ribbing at the end, 72 (76, 80)ftr. Join to work in round.

Rounds 1–4: 3ch, *1RtrF, 1RtrB; rep from * around. Join. 72 (76, 80) sts.

Hat

Round 1: Join CC, 1ch, *1dc into RtrF, 2ch, miss 1RtrB*; rep from * around. Join. 36 (38, 40) dc sts.

Round 2: With MC, 1slst to chsp, 3ch

(counts as 1tr) 2tr into chsp, 1ch, miss 1dc, *3tr into chsp, 1ch, miss 1dc; rep from * around. Join. 108 (114, 120) sts.

Round 3: Switch to CC, 1ch, 1dc into last chsp of previous round, 2ch, miss 3tr, *1dc into chsp, 2ch, miss 3tr; rep from * around. Join.

Work rows 2–3 a total of 8 (8, 9) times (for a less slouchy hat, work fewer repeats).

Crown Decreases

Round 1: 1slst to chsp, 3ch (counts as 1tr) 1tr into chsp, 1ch, miss 1dc, *2tr into chsp, 1ch, miss 1dc; rep from * around. Join. 72 (76, 80) sts.

Round 2: Switch to CC, 1ch, 1dc into last chsp of the previous round, miss 2tr, *1dc into chsp, miss 2tr; rep from * around. Join. Break yarn. 36 (38, 40) dc sts.

Finishing

Using the yarn and needle, sew up the gap at the top of the hat, pulling tight to gather the stitches together. Tie the yarn off to secure. Using the tail left at the beginning foundation round, sew up the gap at the bottom edge of the ribbing.

Make a large pom-pom out of CC (see Techniques, page 21) and sew securely to the top of the hat.

thrummed mittens

A layer of warm unspun wool makes these mittens the softest, cosiest things you have ever put on your hands.

skill level **intermediate**

Size	Baby	Child	Small	Medium	Large
Finished circumference	15cm	17cm	19cm	21cm	25.5cm
Finished length from top to wrist	13.5cm	15cm	16.5cm	17.5cm	20cm
Yarn amount (MC):	100m	140m	170m	210m	260m

This pattern is designed to be worn with 2.5cm positive ease.

materials:

* Main Colour (MC): 1 x 100g hank of Ripples Craft Superwash Merino Sport (100 per cent merino), Assynt Rocks
* Optional: a small amount of Contrast Colour (CC): Ripples Craft Superwash Merino Sport (100 per cent merino), Assynt Lochs
* 50g Ripples Craft BFL Top (100 per cent wool), Assynt Lochs
* 4.5mm hook
* 3.75mm hook
* Stitch marker

yarn review:

This lovely sport-weight superwash merino wool is silky and light with excellent stitch definition.

yarn alternatives:

Brown Sheep Nature Spun Sport for the main body of the mittens
Cascade Magum for the wool tops

tension:

Work 19 sts and 19 rows in thrummed double crochet to measure 10cm square using 4.5mm hook, or size needed to achieve tension.

special techniques:

Making a Thrum

Separate your fibre into a long strip, approximately 1cm wide. Starting at one end, pull a tuft off, about 10cm long. Fold each of the ends into the middle and gently roll the middle of the thrum between your fingers to lightly felt the ends.

Working in a Thrum

Insert the hook into the stitch. Place the middle of the thrum on the hook, folding it in half around the hook. Holding it aside with the same hand that you use to hold your hook, YO, and pull both the YO and the thrum through the stitch. YO again and pull through the loops and the thrum on your hook.

Thrums are worked in every 4th stitch in every 3rd row to create a diagonal pattern. Some judgement will be needed at the start of each thrumming round to ensure even placement.

*If you can't find wool tops, use a single ply aran
or chunky wool yarn.*

instructions:

This section is worked in the round, amigurumi style, with no raising of the rounds or turning. Use a stitch marker to keep track of your rounds.

Thrums are worked on rows 2, 5, 8, 11, 14, 17, 20, 23, 26, 29, 32, 35, 38, 41, 44, 47.

Starting with MC and the larger hook, using a magic loop (see Techniques, page 17), make 2ch and 8dc into the loop.

Top of Mitten

Round 1: *2dc into dc; rep from * around. 16 dc.

Round 2 (thrummed round): *1dc, 2dc into dc; rep from * around. 24 dc.

For size Baby ONLY

Round 3: *11dc, 2dc in dc; rep from * around. 26 (-, -, -, -) dc sts.

For sizes Child, Small, Medium and Large ONLY

Round 3: *2dc, 2dc into dc; rep from * around. - (32, 32, 32, 32) dc sts.

For size Small ONLY

Round 4: *15dc, 2dc into dc; rep from * around. - (-, 34 -, -) dc sts.

For size Medium and Large ONLY

Round 4: *3dc, 2dc into dc; rep from * around. - (- , -, 40, 40) dc sts.

For size Large ONLY

Round 5 (thrummed round): *4dc, 2dc into dc; rep from * around. - (-, -. -, -, 48) dc sts.

Hand

Rounds 1–20 (23, 25, 27, 30): (Remember to thrum on round 5 and every 3rd round.) Work even in pattern. 26 (32, 34, 40, 48) dc sts.

Round 21 (24, 26, 28, 31): 1dc, 5 (5, 7, 7, 8)ch, miss 5 (5, 7, 7, 8), dc in each st around to end. 21 (27, 28, 33, 41) dc sts.

Dc into each st and ch around for 5 (6, 9, 9, 10) rounds. 26 (32, 34, 40, 48) dc sts.

Cuff

Rounds 1–8 (11, 11, 13, 13): With smaller hook, 2ch (does not count as a st), *1RtrF, 1RtrB; rep from * around. Do not turn. Join. 28 (32, 36, 40, 48) sts.

Round 9 (12, 12, 14, 14): If you are working a CC round, switch to CC, 1ch, 28 (32, 36, 40, 48)dc. Join. Break yarn.

Thumb

This section is worked in the round, amigurumi style, with no raising of the rounds or turning. Use a stitch marker to keep track of your rounds.

Rejoin MC at the first missed stitch for the thumbhole. 12 (12, 16, 16, 20)dc around the thumbhole, working across the missed stitches and the chains and into the row ends at each side of the opening. 12 (12, 16, 16, 20) sts.

Rounds 1–7 (8, 9, 10, 11): 12 (12, 16, 16, 20)dc (Thrum rounds 3, 6, and 9 as required), 12 (12, 16, 16, 20) sts.

Round 8 (9, 10, 11, 12): *1dc2tog, 2dc; rep from * around. 9 (9, 12, 12, 15) sts.

Round 9 (10, 11, 12, 13): *1dc2tog, 1dc; rep from * around. 6 (6, 8, 8, 10) sts.

Round 10 (11, 12, 13, 14): 1dctog around. 3 (3, 4, 4, 5) sts.

Finishing

Sew in ends.

buttoned capelet

Worn on its own or under a jacket as a cowl,
this is a very versatile garment.

skill level **intermediate**

Size	Small	Medium	Large	Extra large
Finished circumference at bottom hem	131cm	152cm	172cm	192cm
Finished length from first buttonhole to hem	42cm	44cm	45.5cm	48.5cm
Yarn amount	755m	910m	1075m	1275m

materials:

* 3 (3, 3, 4) x 115g hanks of 4-ply Fyberspates Vivacious (100 per cent merino), Deep Forest
* 3 (3, 3, 4) x buttons approximately 2.5cm diameter
* 4.5mm hook

yarn review:

This slightly variegated sock yarn is very washable and durable.

yarn alternative:

Rowan Fine Nordic Tweed

tension:

Work 19 stitches and 11 rows in linked treble crochet to measure 10cm square using 4.5mm hook, or size required to achieve tension.

special stitches:

Linked Treble Crochet (ltr)

First Stitch after tch:

Insert the hook into the 2nd chain of the turning chain, YO and pull through, insert the hook into the next stitch, YO and pull through, YO, pull the loop through the two loops on the hook, YO, pull through the last two loops.

All other stitches:

Insert the hook into the middle loop of the stitch just worked, YO and pull through, insert the hook into the next stitch, YO and pull through, YO, pull the loop through the two loops on the hook, YO, pull through the last two loops.

Raised Double Crochet Back (RdcB)

Insert the hook from the back of the fabric around the front of the post of the stitch below and then out the back of the fabric, YO and pull through the stitch, YO and pull through the two loops on the hook.

pattern note:

Count the turning chain as a stitch.

The linked treble crochet stitches give this capelet a lot of drape.

Make 82 (82, 101, 101)ch.

Neck Opening

Row 1 (RS): Starting in 4th ch from the hook (counts as 1tr), 78 (78, 97, 97)ltr. Turn. 79 (79, 98, 98) sts.

Rows 2–17: 3ch, 78 (78, 97, 97)ltr. Turn.

Shoulder to Ripple

Row 1 (RS): 3ch, 1ltr, 1ch, miss 1ltr, [2ltr in next ltr, 3 (3, 4, 4)ltr] 19 times. Turn. 97 (97, 116, 116) sts.

Row 2 and all WS rows: Ltr into each ltr and ch across.

Row 3: 3ch, 2ltr, [4 (4, 5, 5)ltr, 2ltr in next ltr] 19 times. Turn. 117 (117, 136, 136) sts.

Row 5: 3ch, 2ltr, [2ltr in next ltr, 5 (5, 6, 6)ltr] 19 times. Turn. 136 (136, 155, 155) sts.

Row 7: 3ch, 2ltr, [6 (6, 7, 7)ltr, 2ltr in next ltr] 19 times. Turn. 155 (155, 174, 174) sts.

Row 9 (buttonhole row): 3ch, 1ltr, 1ch, miss 1ltr, [2ltr in next ltr, 7 (7, 8, 8)ltr] 19 times. Turn. 173 (173, 192, 192) sts.

Row 11: 3ch, 2ltr, [8 (8, 9, 9)ltr, 2ltr in next ltr] 19 times. Turn. 193 (193, 212, 212) sts.

Row 13: 3ch, 2ltr, [2ltr in next ltr, 9 (9, 10, 10)ltr] 19 times. Turn. 212 (212, 231, 231) sts.

Row 15: 3ch, 2ltr, [10 (10, 11, 11)ltr, 2ltr in next ltr] 19 times. Turn. 231 (231, 250, 250) sts.

Row 17 (buttonhole row): 3ch, 1ltr, 1ch, miss 1ltr, [2ltr in next ltr, 11 (11, 12, 12)ltr] 19 times. Turn. 249 (249, 268, 268) sts.

For sizes Medium, Large and Extra Large ONLY

Row 19: 3ch, 2ltr, [- (12, 13, 13)ltr, 2ltr in next ltr] 19 times. Turn. - (269, 288, 288) sts.

Row 21: 3ch, 2ltr, [2ltr in next ltr, - (13, 14, 14)ltr] 19 times. Turn - (288, 307, 307) sts.

For sizes Large and Extra Large ONLY

Row 23: 3ch, 2ltr, [- (-, 15, 15) ltr, 2ltr in next ltr] 19 times. Turn. - (-, 326, 326) sts.

For size Extra Large ONLY

Row 25 (buttonhole row): 3ch, 1ltr, 1ch, miss 1ltr, [2ltr in next ltr, 16ltr] 19 times. Turn. - (-, -, 345) sts.

Row 27: 3ch, 2ltr, [17ltr, 2ltr in next ltr] 19 times. Turn. - (-, -, 364) sts.

ALL Sizes

Work even for 3 (1, 1, -) rows.

Joining for Working in the Round (ALL Sizes):

3ch, place the last 2 sts of the row under the first 3 sts in the row, 3ltr, working through both layers, 244 (282, 320, 358)ltr. Join. Do not turn. 247 (285, 323, 361) sts.

Ripple

Ripple notes:

Do not count the beginning chain as a stitch throughout this section.

Work in rounds with RS facing. Do not turn.

Round 1 (RS) and all odd rows: 1ch, 247 (285, 323, 361)RdcB. Join.

Round 2: 3ch, [5tr in next, (1tr in next, miss 1) eight times, 1tr, 5tr in next] 13 (15, 17, 19) times. Join.

Round 4: 4ch, [5dtr in next, (1dtr in next, miss 1) eight times, 1dtr, 5dtr in next] 13 (15, 17, 19) times. Join. Do not turn.

Round 6: 5ch, [5ttr in next, (1ttr in next, miss 1) eight times, 1ttr, 5ttr in next] 13 (15, 17, 19) times. Join. Do not turn.

Round 8: Repeat round 2.

Round 10: Repeat round 4.

Round 12: Repeat round 6.

Round 14: Repeat round 2.

Round 16: Repeat round 4.

Round 18: Repeat round 6.

Round 19: Repeat round 1.

Finishing

Weave in the ends. Using the buttonholes for placement, sew on the buttons.

waterfall shrug

This oversized cardigan is perfect for wrapping up on a cold day. Its simple construction makes it a perfect first garment.

skill level **beginner**

Size	Extra small	Small	Medium	Large	Extra large
Finished width (a)	124cm	140cm	156cm	172cm	188cm
Finished length (b)	38cm	38cm	48cm	48cm	58cm
Shoulder to shoulder (c)	50cm	59cm	59cm	59cm	75cm
Yarn amount	610m	680m	940m	1030m	1340m

materials:

* 13 (14, 19, 21, 27) x 50g hanks of Artesano Alpaca DK (100 per cent alpaca) in Sweet Pea
* 5mm hook

yarn review:

Light as air and gorgeously drapy, this 100 per cent alpaca DK-weight wool is a joy to work with.

yarn alternative:

Artesano Superwash DK

tension:

16 sts and 8 rows in treble crochet to 10cm square using 5mm hook or size needed to achieve tension.
Tension square of Crossed Shell Stitch (see Special Stitches) measures 12cm x 10cm blocked.

special stitches:

Crossed Shell Stitch (CS):
Instructions for Tension Square:
29ch. (Stitch chart on page 81.)
Set up Row: 3tr in the 5th ch from the hook (tch counts as 1tr and 1ch), miss 3ch, [1dc, miss 5ch, 3tr in next ch, 2ch, working back in to the 2nd ch missed, 3tr, miss 5ch from the stitch just made] twice, 1dc, miss 3ch, (3tr, 1ch, 1tr) into ch. Turn. 2 completed CS sts and 1 half CS at either end.
Row 1: 1ch (does not count as a stitch), 1dc into tr, 3ch, miss 3tr, 1tr into dc, [3ch, miss 3tr, 1dc into 2chsp, 3ch, miss 3tr, 1tr into dc] twice, 3ch, miss 3tr, 1dc into chsp. Turn.

Row 2: 1ch (does not count as a stitch), 1dc into dc, miss 3chsp and 1tr, 3tr into chsp, [2ch, 3tr into missed 3chsp, 1dc into dc, miss 3chsp and 1tr, 3tr into 3chsp] twice, 2ch, 3tr into missed 3chsp, 1dc into dc. Turn.

Row 3: 6ch (counts as 1tr and 3ch), miss 3tr, 1dc into 2chsp, [3ch, miss 3tr, 1tr into dc, miss 3tr, 1dc into 2chsp] twice, 3ch, miss 3tr, 1tr in dc. Turn.

Row 4: 4ch (counts as 1tr and 3ch), 3tr in tr, miss 3ch, [1dc in dc, miss 3ch and 1tr, 3tr into 3chsp, 2ch, 3tr into missed 3chsp] 4 times, 1dc into dc, miss 3ch, (3tr, 1ch, 1tr) into ch. Turn.

Work rows 1–4 twice. Wash and block for tension.

pattern notes:

When crossing your stitches, work in front of the 3tr group you have already made.

instructions:

Body:

261 (293, 325, 357, 389)ch.

Set up Row (RS): 3tr in the 5th ch from the hook (t-ch counts as 1tr and 1ch), miss 3ch, [1dc, miss 5ch, 3tr in next ch, 2ch, working back in to the 2nd ch missed, 3tr, miss 5ch from the stitch just made] 31 (35, 39, 43, 47) times, 1dc, miss 3ch, (3tr, 1ch, 1tr) into ch. Turn. 31 (35, 39, 43, 47) CS sts.

Row 1: 1ch (does not count as a stitch), 1dc into tr, 3ch, miss 3tr, 1tr into dc, [3ch, miss 3tr, 1dc into 2chsp, 3ch, miss 3tr, 1tr into dc] 31 (35, 39, 43, 47) times, 3ch, miss 3tr, 1dc into chsp. Turn. 32 (36, 40, 44, 48) tr sts.

Row 2: 1ch (does not count as a stitch), 1dc into dc, miss 3chsp and 1tr, 3tr into chsp, [2ch, 3tr into missed 3chsp, 1dc into dc, miss 3chsp and 1tr, 3tr into 3chsp] 31 (35, 39, 43, 47) times, 2ch, 3tr into missed 3chsp, 1dc into dc. Turn. 32 (36, 40, 44, 48) CS sts.

Row 3: 6ch (counts as 1tr and 3ch), miss 3tr, 1dc into 2chsp, [3ch, miss 3tr, 1tr into dc, miss 3tr, 1dc into 2chsp] 31 (35, 39, 43, 47) times, 3ch, miss 3tr, 1tr in dc. Turn. 33 (37, 41, 45, 49) tr sts.

Row 4: 4ch (counts as 1tr and 3ch), 3tr in tr, miss 3ch and 1tr, [3tr into 3chsp, 2ch, 3tr into missed 3chsp, 1dc in dc, miss 3ch and 1tr] 31 (35, 39, 43, 47) times, 1dc into dc, miss 3ch, (3tr, 1ch, 1tr) into ch. Turn. 31 (35, 39, 43, 47) CS sts.

Work rows 1–4 a total of 3 (3, 4, 4, 5) times.

Work rows 1–2 once more.

Armholes:

Armhole Row 1: 6ch (counts as 1tr and 3ch), miss 3tr, 1dc into 2chsp, [3ch, miss 3tr, 1tr into dc, miss 3tr, 1dc into 2chsp] 8 (9, 10, 12, 12) times, 24 (32, 32, 32, 32) ch, miss 2 (2, 3, 3, 3) CS, 1dc into the next 2chsp, [3ch, miss 3tr, 1tr into dc, miss 3tr, 1dc into 2chsp] 12 (14, 14, 14) times, 24 (32, 32, 32, 32) ch, miss 2 (2, 3, 3, 3) CS, 1dc into the next 2chsp, [3ch, miss 3tr, 1tr into dc, miss 3tr, 1dc into 2chsp] 8 (9, 10, 12, 12) times, 3ch, miss 3tr, 1tr in dc. Turn.

Armhole Row 2: 4ch (counts as 1tr and 3ch), 3tr in tr, miss 3ch and 1tr, [3tr into 3chsp, 2ch, 3tr into missed 3chsp, 1dc in dc, miss 3ch and 1tr] 8 (9, 10, 12, 12) times, [1dc into ch, miss 5ch, 3tr in next ch, 2ch, working back in to the 2nd ch missed, 3tr, miss 1ch] 3 (3, 4, 4, 4) times, [1dc in dc, miss 3ch and 1tr, 3tr into 3chsp, 2ch, 3tr into missed 3chsp] 11 (13, 13, 13, 17) times, [1dc into ch, miss 5ch, 3tr in next ch, 2ch, working back in to the 2nd ch missed, 3tr, miss 1ch] 3 (4, 4, 4, 4) times, [1dc in dc, miss 3ch and 1tr, 3tr into 3chsp, 2ch, 3tr into missed 3chsp] 8 (9, 10, 12, 12) times, 1dc into dc, miss 3ch, (3tr, 1ch, 1tr) into ch. Turn. 31 (35, 39, 43, 47) CS sts.

Work body rows 1–4 a total of 3 (3, 4, 4, 5) times.

Work row 1 once more.

The stitch pattern looks complicated at first, but after the set up rows it is easily memorised.

Edging:

Round 1: 3ch, 258 (289, 321, 353, 385) tr, working into each stitch and chain across, (1tr, 2ch, 1tr) into corner stitch, working into the row ends, 60 (60, 76, 76, 92) tr evenly spaced across, (1tr, 2ch, 1tr) into corner stitch, working into the beg-ch, 256 (288, 320, 352, 384) tr, (1tr, 2ch, 1tr) into corner stitch, working into the row ends, 60 (60, 76, 76, 92) tr evenly spaced across, (1tr, 2ch, 1tr) into corner stitch. Join. 640 (704, 800, 864, 960) sts.

Break yarn. Block rectangle to open up the lace.

Sleeves (Make 2):

Set Up Row: With RS facing, reattach yarn at the dc at the edge of the armhole, working into the missed stitches of Armhole Row 1, [3ch, miss 3tr, 1tr into dc, miss 3tr, 1dc into 2ch-sp] 3 (3, 4, 4, 4) times.

Round 1: 3 ch (counts as 1tr), working across the chain from round 15, 24 (24, 32, 32, 32) tr, 1tr into each st and ch of the sleeve set-up. Join. 48 (48, 64, 64, 64) sts.

Rounds 2–24 (25, 26, 27, 27): 3ch (counts as 1tr), 47 (47, 63, 63, 63) tr. Join. 48 (48, 64, 64, 64) sts.

Break yarn. Weave in ends.

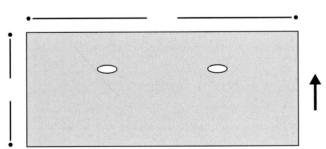

abbreviated sample of stitch pattern

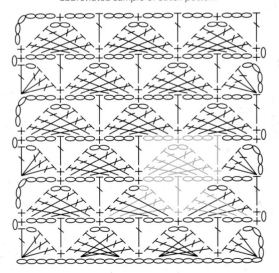

○ chain

┬ treble crochet

┬ double crochet

wedding bells

The perfect gift for a bride or bridal party, this pretty wrap will do its best to prevent cold shoulders, if not cold feet!

skill level **advanced**

Size	Small	Medium	Large	Extra large
Finished bottom circumference	101cm	127cm	152cm	177cm
Finished length from neck to hem	34cm	34cm	34cm	34cm
Yarn amount	470m	590m	705m	820m

Each size will fit a large range of chest sizes.

materials:
* 3 (4, 4, 5) x 50g hanks of 4-ply Artesano (100 per cent alpaca), Cream
* 4.5mm hook
* 60cm x 1cm wide ribbon

yarn review:
This 4-ply yarn is soft and elegant with the characteristic drape and slight halo of 100 per cent alpaca.

yarn alternative:
Debbie Bliss Rialto
Artesano 4-ply

tension:
Work 18 stitches and 11 rows in linked treble crochet to measure 10cm square using 4.5mm hook, or size needed to achieve tension.

special stitch:
Linked Treble Crochet (ltr)
First Stitch after tch:
Insert the hook into the 2nd chain of the turning chain, YO and pull through, insert the hook into the next stitch, YO and pull through, YO, pull the loop through two loops on the hook, YO, pull through the last two loops.

All other stitches:
Insert the hook into the middle loop of the stitch just worked, YO and pull through, insert the hook into the next stitch, YO and pull through, YO, pull the loop through two loops on the hook, YO, pull through the last two loops.

pattern notes:

Do not count the tch at the beginning of the rows as a stitch.

The shawl is worked in two parts out from either side of the beginning chain, which acts as the central back seam.

When working short rows, turn your work before the end of the row. As the rows get longer and you pass the step created by the previous short rows, work the first stitch as follows:

Insert the hook into the middle loop of the stitch just worked, YO and pull through, insert the hook into the 2nd chain of tch one row below, YO and pull through, insert the hook through the middle bar of the stitch two rows below, YO and pull through, insert the hook into the next stitch, YO and pull through, YO and pull through four loops on the hook. YO and pull through all loops on the hook.

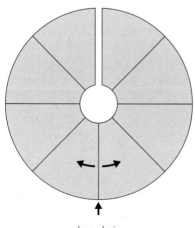

beg chain

abbreviated sample of stitch pattern

○ *chain*

┬ *treble*

┖ *raised treble*

instructions:

Make 77ch.

Right Panel

Row 1 (RS): Starting in 4th ch from hook, 3tr in next, [miss 3ch, 2tr, 1ch, miss 1ch, 2tr, miss 3ch, (3tr, 1ch, 3tr) in next] twice, miss 3ch, 2tr, 1ch, miss 1ch, 2tr, miss 3ch, 3tr in next, 1ch, miss 1ch, 1tr, 35ltr. Turn. 66 sts.

Row 2 (WS): 3ch, 35ltr, 1RtrB, 1ch, 3tr in chsp, [miss 3tr, 2RtrB, 1ch, 2RtrB, miss 3tr, (3tr, 1ch, 3tr) in chsp] twice, miss 3tr, 2tr, 1ch, miss 1tr, 2tr, miss 3tr, 3tr in chsp, 1tr in tch. Turn. 67 sts.

Row 3: 4ch, 3tr in chsp, [miss 3tr, 2RtrF, 1ch, 2RtrF, miss 3tr, (3tr, 1ch, 3tr) in chsp] twice, miss 3tr, 2tr, 1ch, miss 1tr, 2tr, miss 3tr, 3tr in chsp, 1RtrF. Turn. 31sts.

Row 4: 4ch, 2tr, [miss 3tr, 2RtrB, (1tr, 1ch, 1tr) in chsp, 2RtrB, miss 3tr, (2tr, 1ch, 2tr) in chsp] twice, miss 3tr, 2RtrB, (1tr, 1ch, 1tr) in chsp, 2RtrB, miss 3tr, 1tr in chsp, 1ch, 1tr in tch. Turn. 30 sts.

Row 5: 4ch, miss (1tr, 1ch, 1tr), 2RtrF, [miss 1tr, (3tr, 1ch, 3tr) in chsp, miss 1tr, 2RtrF 1ch, miss (2tr, 1ch, 2tr), 2RtrF] twice, miss 1tr, (3tr, 1ch, 3tr) in chsp, miss 1tr, 2RtrF, 1ch, miss 2tr, 1RtrF in tch, 7ltr. Turn. 38 sts.

Row 6: 3ch, 7ltr, 1RtrB, 1ch, 2RtrB, [miss 3tr, (3tr, 1ch, 3tr) in chsp, miss 3tr, 2RtrB, 1ch, 2RtrB] twice, miss 3tr, (3tr, 1ch, 3tr) in chsp, miss 3tr, 2RtrB, 1ch, 1tr in tch. Turn. 39 sts.

Row 7: 4ch, 2RtrF, [miss 3tr, (3tr, 1ch, 3tr) in chsp, miss 3tr, 2RtrF, 1ch, 2RtrF] twice, miss 3tr, (3tr, 1ch, 3tr) in chsp, miss 3tr, 2RtrF, 1ch, 1RtrF, 14ltr. Turn. 46 sts.

Row 8: 3ch, 14ltr, 1RtrB, 1ch, 2RtrB, [miss 3tr, (3tr, 1ch, 3tr) in chsp, miss 3tr, 2RtrB, 1ch, 2RtrB] twice, miss 3tr, (3tr, 1ch, 3tr) in chsp, miss 3tr, 2RtrB, 1ch, 1tr in tch. Turn.

Row 9: 4ch, 2RtrF, [miss 3tr, (3tr, 1ch, 3tr) in chsp, miss 3tr, 2RtrF, 1ch, 2RtrF] twice, miss 3tr, (3tr, 1ch, 3tr) in chsp, miss 3tr, 2RtrF, 1ch, 1RtrF, 21ltr. Turn. 52 sts.

Row 10: 3ch, 21ltr, 1RtrB, 1tr in chsp, 2RtrB, [miss 3tr, (2tr, 1ch, 2tr) in chsp, miss 3tr, 2RtrB, (1tr, 1ch, 1tr) in chsp, 2RtrB] twice, miss 3tr, (2tr, 1ch, 2tr) in chsp, miss 3tr, 2RtrB, 1tr in chsp, 1ch, miss 1RtrF, 1tr in tch. Turn. 53 sts.

Row 11: 4ch (counts as 1tr and 1ch), miss 1tr, 3tr in chsp, [2RtrF, 1ch, miss (2tr, 1ch, 2tr), 2RtrF, miss 1tr, (3tr, 1ch, 3tr) in chsp] twice, 2RtrF, 1ch, miss (2tr, 1ch, 2tr), 2RtrF,

For a summer wedding, make this in bamboo or silk for a lightweight wrap, or for a winter wedding, why not try angora?

miss 1tr, 3tr in chsp, 1ch, 1RtrF, 35ltr. Turn. 66 sts.

Row 12: 3ch, 35ltr, 1RtrB, 3tr in chsp, [miss 3tr, 2RtrB, 1ch, 2RtrB, miss 3tr, (3tr, 1ch, 3tr) in chsp] twice, miss 3tr, 2RtrB, 1ch, miss 1RtrB, 2tr, miss 3tr, 3tr in chsp, 1tr in tch. Turn. 67 sts.

Row 13: 4ch, 3tr, [miss 3tr, 2RtrF, 1ch, 2RtrF, miss 3tr, (3tr, 1ch, 3tr) in chsp] twice, miss 3tr, 2tr, 1ch, miss 1tr, 2tr, miss 3tr, 3tr in chsp, 1RtrF, 35ltr. Turn.

Work rows 2–13 a total of 4 (5, 6, 7) times.

Ribbon Hole Row

3ch, 7ltr, 1ch, miss one, 27ltr, 1RtrB, 1ch, 3tr in chsp, [miss 3tr, 2RtrB, 1ch, 2RtrB, miss 3tr, (3tr, 1ch, 3tr) in chsp] twice, miss 3tr, 2tr, 1ch, miss 1tr, 2tr, miss 3tr, 3tr in chsp, 1tr in tch. Turn. Break yarn.

Left Panel

Row 1 (WS): Rejoin yarn onto beg ch at cabled end, WS facing. Working into unworked side of beg ch, 4ch, 3tr in next, [miss 3tr, 2tr, 1ch, miss 1tr, 2tr, miss 3tr, (3tr, 1ch, 3tr) in next] twice, miss 3tr, 2tr, 1ch, miss 1tr, 2tr, miss 3tr, 3tr in next, 1ch, miss one, 1tr, 35ltr. Turn. 66 sts.

Row 2 (RS): 3ch, 35ltr, 1RtrF, 1ch, 3tr in chsp, [miss 3tr, 2RtrF, 1ch, 2RtrF, miss 3tr, (3tr, 1ch, 3tr) in chsp] twice, miss 3tr, 2tr,

1ch, miss 1tr, 2tr, miss 3tr, 3tr in chsp, 1tr in tch. Turn. 67 sts.

Row 3: 4ch, 3tr in chsp, [miss 3tr, 2RtrB, 1ch, 2RtrB, miss 3tr, (3tr, 1ch, 3tr) in chsp] twice, miss 3tr, 2tr, 1ch, miss 1tr, 2tr, miss 3tr, 3tr in chsp, 1RtrB. Turn. 31sts.

Row 4: 4ch, 2tr in chsp, [miss 3tr, 2RtrF, (1tr, 1ch, 1tr) in chsp, 2RtrF, miss 3tr, (2tr, 1ch, 2tr) in chsp] twice, miss 3tr, 2RtrF, (1tr, 1ch, 1tr) in chsp, 2RtrF, miss 3tr, 1tr in chsp, 1ch, 1tr in tch. 30 sts.

Row 5: 4ch, miss (1tr, 1ch, 1tr), 2RtrB, [miss 1tr, (3tr, 1ch, 3tr) in chsp, miss 1tr, 2RtrB, 1ch, miss (2tr, 1ch, 2tr), 2RtrB] twice, miss 1tr, (3tr, 1ch, 3tr) in chsp, miss 1tr, 2RtrB, 1ch, miss 2tr, 1RtrB, 7ltr. Turn. 38 sts.

Row 6: 3ch, 7ltr, 1RtrF, 1ch, 2RtrF, [miss 3tr, (3tr, 1ch, 3tr) in chsp, miss 3tr, 2RtrF, 1ch, 2RtrF] twice, miss 3tr, (3tr, 1ch, 3tr) in chsp, miss 3tr, 2RtrB, 1ch, 1tr in tch. Turn. 39 sts.

Row 7: 4ch, 2RtrB, [miss 3tr, (3tr, 1ch, 3tr) in chsp, miss 3tr, 2RtrB, 1ch, 2RtrB] twice, miss 3tr, (3tr, 1ch, 3tr) in chsp, miss 3tr, 2RtrB, 1ch, 1RtrB, 14ltr. Turn. 45 sts.

Row 8: 3ch, 14ltr, 1RtrF, 1ch, 2RtrF, [miss 3tr, (3tr, 1ch, 3tr) in chsp, miss 3tr, 2RtrF, 1ch, 2RtrF] twice, miss 3tr, (3tr, 1ch, 3tr) in chsp, miss 3tr, 2RtrB, 1ch, 1tr in tch. Turn.

Row 9: 4ch, 2RtrB [miss 3tr, (3tr, 1ch, 3tr) in chsp, miss 3tr, 2RtrB, 1ch, 2RtrB] twice, miss 3tr, (3tr, 1ch, 3tr) in chsp, miss 3tr, 2RtrB,

1ch, 1RtrB, 21ltr. Turn. 52 sts.

Row 10: 3ch, 21ltr, 1RtrF, 1tr in chsp, 2RtrF, [miss 3tr, (2tr, 1ch, 2tr) in chsp, miss 3tr, 2RtrF, (1tr, 1ch, 1tr) in chsp, 2RtrF] twice, miss 3tr, (2tr, 1ch, 2tr) in chsp, miss 3tr, 2RtrF, 1tr in chsp, 1ch, 1tr in tch. Turn. 53 sts.

Row 11: 4ch, 3tr in chsp, [2RtrB, 1ch, miss (2tr, 1ch, 2tr), 2RtrB, miss 1tr, (3tr, 1ch, 3tr) in chsp] twice, 2RtrB, 1ch, miss (2tr, 1ch, 2tr), 2RtrB, miss 1tr, 3tr in chsp, 1ch, 1RtrB, 35ltr. Turn. 66 sts.

Row 12: 3ch, 35ltr, 1RtrF, 3tr in chsp, [miss 3tr, 2RtrF, 1ch, 2RtrF, miss 3tr, (3tr, 1ch, 3tr) in chsp] twice, miss 3tr, 2tr, 1ch, miss 1tr, 2tr, miss 3tr, 3tr in chsp, 1tr in tch. Turn. 67 sts.

Row 13: 4ch, 3tr in chsp, [miss 3tr, 2RtrB, 1ch, 2RtrB, miss 3tr, (3tr, 1ch, 3tr) in chsp] twice, miss 3tr, 2tr, 1ch, miss 1tr, 2tr, miss 3tr, 3tr in chsp, 1RtrB, 35ltr. Turn.

Work rows 2–13 a total of 4 (5, 6, 7) times.

Ribbon Hole Row

3ch, 7ltr, 1ch, miss one, 27ltr, 1RtrF, 1ch, 3tr in chsp, [miss 3tr, 2RtrF, 1ch, 2RtrF, miss 3tr, (3tr, 1ch, 3tr) in chsp,] twice, miss 3tr, 2tr, 1ch, miss 1tr, 2tr, miss 3tr, 3tr in chsp, 1tr in tch. Turn.

Finishing

Break yarn. Block. Thread the ribbon through the holes and tie off to close.

 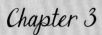

Chapter 3

For Him

* * * * * * *

Knitterly hat

Knitterly cowl

Granite mitts

Leather and linen tablet case

Everyone (needs) socks

Shawl collar cardigan

knitterly hat

A simple change to a basic half treble crochet creates a gender neutral fabric, with a 'knit look' stitch.

skill level **beginner**

Size	Newborn	Baby	Toddler	Child	Adult
Finished brim circumference	36cm	42cm	47cm	53cm	60cm
Finished height	13cm	15cm	17cm	19cm	23cm
Yarn amount	90m	125m	155m	200m	255m

Designed to be worn with 0cm negative ease.

materials:

* 1 (1, 2, 2, 2) x 100g hanks of Malabrigo Twist (100 per cent wool), Terron
* 6.5mm hook

yarn review:

This chunky-weight yarn lives up to its name, with great twist, making it hard-wearing with beautiful stitch definition.

yarn alternative:

Wendy Mode Chunky

tension:

Work 13.5 sts and 11 rows in half treble crochet in the back bar to measure 10cm square using 6.5mm hook, or size needed to achieve tension.

special stitches:

Half Treble Crochet in the Back Bar (htrb)
YO the hook, insert the hook into the bar behind the back loop, YO and pull through the stitch (three loops on the hook), YO and pull through all the loops on the hook.

Half Treble Crochet in the Front Bar (htrf)
YO the hook, insert the hook into the bar in front of the front loop, YO and pull through the stitch (three loops on the hook), YO and pull through all loops on the hook.

pattern notes:

The hat is worked from the top down in rounds. Do not count the tch at the beginning of the round as a stitch. Most of the hat is worked with the WS facing; do not turn the rounds unless specified.

instructions:

Round 1 (WS): Working into magic loop (see Techniques, page 17), 2ch, 8htr. Join.

Round 2: 2ch, *2htrb in next; rep from * around. Join. 16 sts.

Round 3: 2ch, *1htrb, 2htrb in next; rep from * around. Join. 24 sts.

Round 4: 2ch, *2htrb, 2htrb in next; rep from * around. Join. 32 sts.

Round 5: 2ch, *3htrb, 2htrb in next; rep from * around. Join. 40 sts.

Round 6: 2ch, *4htrb, 2htrb in next; rep from * around. Join. 48 sts.

For sizes Baby, Toddler, Child and Adult ONLY

Round 7: 2ch, *5htrb, 2htrb in next; rep from * around. Join. 56 sts.

For sizes Toddler, Child and Adult ONLY

Round 8: 2ch, *6htrb, 2htrb in next; rep from * around. Join. 64 sts.

For sizes Child and Adult ONLY

Round 9: 2ch, *7htrb, 2htrb in next; rep from * around. Join. 72 sts.

For size Adult ONLY

Round 10: 2ch, *8htrb, 2htrb in next; rep from * around. Join. 80 sts.

For ALL sizes

Round 1: 2ch, 48 (56, 64, 72, 80)htrb. Join. 48 (56, 64, 72, 80) sts.

Work round 1 a total of 2 (4, 5, 0, 3) times.

Pattern:

Round 1: Turn. 2ch, 48 (56, 64, 72, 80)htrf. Join. Do not turn.

Round 2: 2ch, 48 (56, 64, 72, 80)htrb. Join. Do not turn.

Round 3: 2ch, 48 (56, 64, 72, 80)htrb. Join. Turn.

Work rounds 1–3 a total of 2 (2, 2, 4, 4) times.

Finishing

Block and weave in ends.

For a bolder 'stripe' of stitches, turn your work
earlier to create a larger band of knit-look ridges.

knitterly cowl

This cowl is very chunky, very warm and guaranteed to keep its recipient snuggly in the coldest of weathers.

skill level **beginner**

Size	One size
Finished height	32cm
Finished circumference	70cm
Yarn amount	340m

materials:

* 3 x 100g hanks Malabrigo Twist (100 per cent wool), Terron
* 6.5mm hook

yarn review:

This is a beautiful chunky-weight yarn with a soft touch and crystal clear stitch definition.

yarn alternatives:

Wendy Mode Chunky

tension:

Work 13.5 sts and 11 rows in half treble crochet in the back bar to measure 10cm square using 6.5mm hook, or size needed to achieve tension.

special stitches:

Half Treble Crochet in the Back Bar (htrb)
YO the hook, insert the hook into the bar behind the back loop, YO and pull through the stitch (three loops on the hook), YO and pull through all the loops on the hook.

Half Treble Crochet in the Front Bar (htrf)
YO the hook, insert the hook into the bar in front of the front loop, YO and pull through the stitch (three loops on the hook), YO and pull through all the loops on the hook.

pattern notes:

Count the tch at the beginning of the round as a stitch.

There is no RS or WS to the pattern, with the stitch pattern being reversible.

instructions:

Make 95ch. Join for working in the round, being careful not to twist.

Round 1 (RS): 2ch, 95htr. Join. Do not turn.

Round 2: 2ch, 95htrb. Join. Do not turn.

Round 3: 2ch, 95htrb. Join. Turn.

Round 4: 2ch, 95htrf. Join. Do not turn.

Round 5: 2ch, 95htrb. Join. Do not turn.

Round 6: 2ch, 95htrb. Join. Turn.

Work rounds 4–6 until the piece measures 32cm from the beginning chain.

Finishing

Weave in the ends and block.

This pattern is easily adaptable. Chain a length you want the cowl. Join in the round and work in pattern until your cowl is wide enough.

granite mitts

The reverse side of the common granite stitch is perfect for more unisex gifts. Combined with a silk blend yarn, these mitts are perfect for the refined men in your life.

skill level **beginner**

Size	Small	Medium	Large	Extra large
Finished circumference (a)	15cm	17.5cm	18.5cm	20cm
Finished length (b)	15cm	18cm	20cm	23cm
Yarn amount	130m	160m	200m	250m

Designed to be worn with 2cm negative ease.

materials:
* 1 x 100g hank Cascade Venezia Sport, (70 per cent merino wool, 30 per cent mulberry silk), Ginger (160)
* 3.75mm hook
* Stitch marker

yarn review:
A light and drapey sport-weight, this yarn has just a hint of sheen.

yarn alternative:
MillaMia Naturally Soft Merino

tension:
Work 13 sts and 26 rows in granite stitch to measure 10cm square using 3.75mm hook, or size needed to achieve tension.

special stitch:
Granite Stitch (for swatch)
Chain an even number of stitches.
Row 1: Starting with 2nd ch from hook, 1dc *1ch, miss 1ch, 1dc in the next ch; rep from * to last 2ch. 2 dc. Turn.
Row 2: 1ch, 1dc, 1ch, miss next dc, *1dc in next chsp, 1ch, miss next dc; to last 2 sts, 1dc in chsp, 1dc in dc. Turn.
Work row 2 until the piece measures at least 10cm from the beginning chain.

pattern note:
This pattern is worked in the round in the amigurumi style, with no seams or turning chains at the start of the rounds.

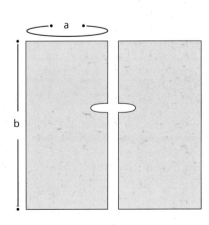

instructions:

Make 40 (44, 48, 52)ch. Join for working in the round, being careful not to twist.

Round 1: 1ch (does not count as a st), 1dc in same st, 1ch, miss next ch, *1dc in next ch, 1ch, miss next ch; rep from * around, pm. Do not join. Do not turn. 20 (22, 24, 26) dc sts.

Round 2: *Miss next dc, 1ch, 1dc in next chsp; rep from * around.

Work round 2 until the piece measures 7.5 (9, 10, 11.5)cm, moving the stitch marker up with each round to mark the start of the round.

Thumb Opening

Round 1: 8 (8, 10, 10)ch, miss next 4 (4, 5, 5)dc and 3 (3, 4, 4)ch, 1dc in next chsp, *miss next dc, 1ch, 1dc in next chsp; rep from * around. 16 (18, 19, 21) dc sts.

Round 2: [1dc in ch, 1ch, miss next ch] 4 (4, 5, 5) times, *miss next dc, 1ch, 1dc in next chsp; rep from * around. 20 (22, 24, 26) dc sts.

Round 3: *Miss next dc, 1ch, 1dc in next chsp; rep from * around.

Work round 3 until the piece measures 15 (18, 20, 23)cm from the top, moving the stitch marker up with each round to mark the start of the round.

Finishing

To finish, slip stitch into the next dc. Break yarn. Turn the mitts inside out and weave in the ends.

The stitch is shown with the wrong side facing. Simply make your tube as you normally would and turn the piece inside out at the end.

leather and linen tablet case

There is just something about the combination of leather and yarn. This most basic of Tunisian stitches works beautifully with the leather, making a perfect gift.

skill level **beginner**

Size	Small	Large
Finished height	20cm	24cm
Finished width	13.5cm	18cm
Yarn amount	70m	120m

materials:

* 1 x 100g hank of Rowan Creative Linen (50 per cent linen, 50 per cent cotton), Natural
* 5mm Tunisian hook
* Leather punch
* 2 x 3cm wide leather buckle or belt

yarn review:

This DK-weight linen cotton blend is hard-wearing and washable. It comes in a range of muted colours.

yarn alternative:

King Cole Craft Cotton

tension:

Work 18 sts and 16 rows in Tunisian simple stitch to measure 10cm square using 5mm hook, or size needed to achieve tension.

special stitches:

See Techniques, page 18 for Tunisian simple stitch (tss) and Standard return pass (srp).

Recycle an old leather belt for the strap.

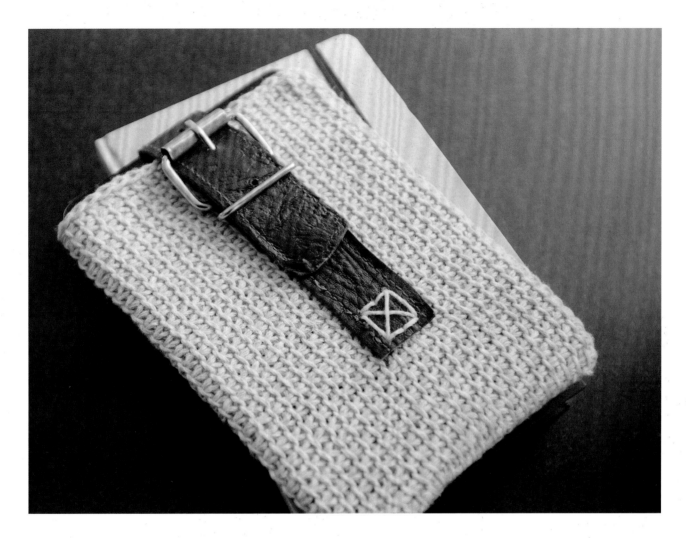

instructions:

Make 49 (65)ch.

Row 1: Starting in 2nd ch from hook, 48 (64)tss, srp. 48 (64) sts.

Row 2: 48 (64)tss, srp.

Work row 2 until the piece measures 20 (24)cm.

With the yarn still attached, fold the work in half, WS together. Working through both layers of fabric, slip stitch the seam closed by working through the larger gaps left in between each tss. Break yarn.

Reattach the yarn at the side seam. Slip stitch the side seam closed. For the neatest finish, insert the hook into both sets of 'chain' loops running along the edges of the rows. Break yarn.

Straps

Using a leather punch on the smallest setting, punch holes around the outside of the bottom of the straps as shown. Sew the strap into place using the photos as a guide – sewing one onto each side of the case.

everyone (needs) socks

Don't just make socks for him. This pattern is sized
so you can make socks for, well, everyone!

skill level **intermediate**

Children

Size	6–12 months	1–3 years	3–5 years	5–7 years	7–13 years
Finished ankle size (a)	10cm	14cm	14cm	16.5cm	18cm
Finished foot length (b)	10cm	13cm	15cm	16cm	18cm
Yarn amount	110m	220m	220m	280m	340m

	Women			Men			
Size	Small	Medium	Large	9	10	11	12
Finished ankle size (a)	18cm	20cm	22.5cm	18cm	20cm	22.5cm	26.5cm
Finished foot length (b)	23cm	25cm	28cm	24cm	26.5cm	28cm	29cm
Yarn amount	410m	500m	580m	430m	520m	600m	740m

Socks are designed to fit with 0–1cm negative ease.

materials:

* 1 (1, 1, 1, 1), 2 (2, 2, 2, 2, 2, 2) hanks
  of Artesano Definition Sock Yarn (75 per
  cent wool, 25 per cent nylon), Tornado
* 3mm hook
* 2 stitch markers

yarn review:

The nylon in this sock-weight yarn makes
it perfect for creating socks you can wear
every day.

yarn alternative:

Regia 6-ply Sock Yarn

tension:

Work 20 sts and 20 rows in extended double
crochet to measure 10cm square using 3mm
hook, or size needed to achieve tension.

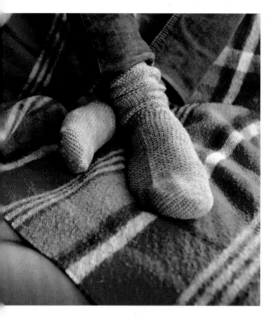

Nothing says 'I love you' more than taking the time to make something as everyday as a pair of socks.

special stitch:

Extended Double Crochet (exdc)

Insert the hook into the stitch, YO, pull through, YO, pull through the first loop on the hook, YO, pull through both loops on the hook.

pattern notes:

Do not count the tch as a stitch.
Directions for the adult sizes are shown in bold.

instructions (make 2):

Toe

Make 5 (5, 7, 7, 9), **9 (11, 13, 11, 13, 13, 13)**ch.

Round 1: 1ch, 2dc in 2nd chain from hook, 2 (2, 4, 4, 6), **6 (8, 10, 8, 10, 10, 10)**dc, (2dc, pm, 2dc) into last ch turning work as you go to work across other side of beg ch, 2 (2, 4, 4, 6), **6 (8, 10, 8, 10, 10, 10)**dc, 2dc in last ch, pm. Join. 12 (12, 16, 16, 20), **20 (24, 28, 24, 28, 28, 28)** sts.

Round 2: 1ch, 2dc in first st, dc to 1 st before marker, 2dc in dc, sm, 2dc in dc, dc to 1 st before end of round, 2dc in dc. Join. 16 (16, 20, 20, 24), **24 (28, 32, 28, 32, 32, 32)** sts.
Work round 2 a total of 2 (4, 3, 4, 4), **4 (4, 4, 3, 3, 4, 6)** times. 20 (28, 28, 32, 36), **36 (40, 44, 36, 40, 44, 52)** sts.

Foot

Round 1: 2ch, 20 (28, 28, 32, 36), **36 (40, 44, 36, 40, 44, 52)**exdc. Join.
Work round 1 until the piece measures 7 (10, 12, 13.5, 15), **20 (22.5, 25, 21, 23.5, 25, 26)** cm from the toe.

Leg

Round 1: 2ch, 10 (14, 14, 16, 18), **18 (20, 22, 18, 20, 22, 26)**exdc, 10 (14, 14, 16, 18), **18 (20, 22, 18, 20, 22, 26)**fdc, miss 10 (14, 16, 18), **18 (20, 22, 18, 20, 22, 26)**exdc. Join.

Round 2: 2ch, exdc in each fdc and exdc across. 20 (28, 28, 32, 36), **36 (40, 44, 36, 40, 44, 52)** sts.
Work round 2 until the leg measures 7.5 (9, 10, 11.5, 12.5), **14 (14, 14, 14, 15, 15, 15)**cm.

Ribbing

For Children's sizes ONLY

Make 3ch.

Row 1: Starting in 2nd ch from hook, 3dc, slst into next 2 sts of leg. Turn. 3 sts.

Row 2: 3dc in BLO. Turn.

Row 3: 1ch, 3dc in BLO, slst into next 2 sts of leg. Turn.

Continue working rows 2–3 around the leg until all the stitches are used. Slip stitch into the unworked side of the ribbing beginning chain to close. Break yarn.

For Adult sizes ONLY

Make 6ch.

Row 1: Starting in 2nd ch from hook, 6dc, slst into next 2 sts of leg. Turn. 6 sts.

Row 2: 6dc in BLO. Turn.

Row 3: 1ch, 6dc in BLO, slst into next 2 sts of leg. Turn.

Continue working rows 2–3 around the leg until all the stitches are used. Slip stitch into

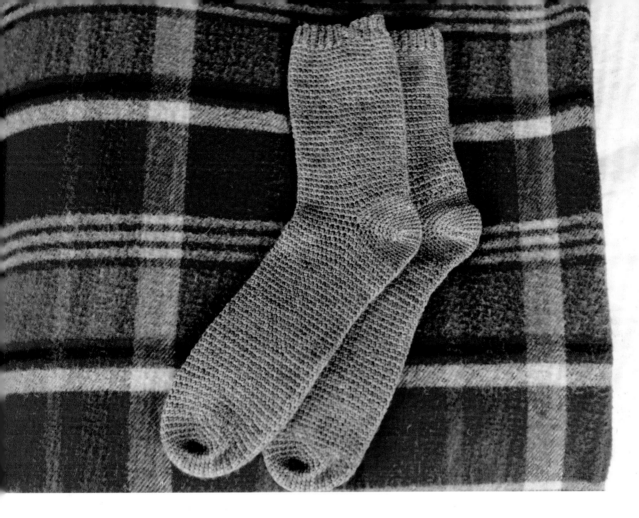

the unworked side of the beginning chain to close. Break yarn.

Afterthought Heel

Rejoin yarn at the first missed stitch of the gusset at the heel.

Round 1: 2ch (does not count as a st), 10 (14, 14, 16, 18), **18 (20, 22, 18, 20, 22, 26)** dc, pm, 10 (14, 14, 16, 18), **18 (20, 22, 18, 20, 22, 26)**dc, pm. Join. 20 (28, 28, 32, 36), **36 (40, 44, 36, 40, 44, 52)** sts.

Round 2: 1ch, 1dc2tog, dc to 2 sts before marker, 1dc2tog, sm, 1dc2tog, dc to 2 sts

before end of round, 1dc2tog. Join. 16 (24, 24, 28, 32), **32 (36, 40, 32, 36, 40, 48)** sts.

Round 3: Work even in pattern.

Work round 2 and 3 a total of 2 (4, 3, 4, 4), **4 (4, 4, 3, 3, 4, 6)** times. 12 (12, 16, 16, 20), **20 (24, 28, 24, 28, 28, 28)** sts.

Finishing

Turn the sock inside out. Fold the heel in half with stitch markers at the corner, rm, sew or slip stitch the heel seam closed. Weave in the ends.

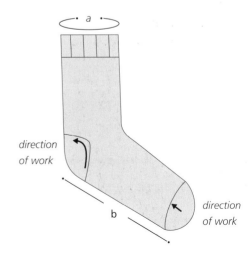

direction of work

direction of work

a

b

shawl collar cardigan

This classic raglan shape with a nice thick shawl collar
is the perfect gift for the men in your life.

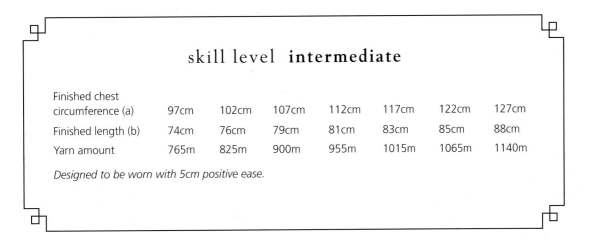

skill level **intermediate**

Finished chest circumference (a)	97cm	102cm	107cm	112cm	117cm	122cm	127cm
Finished length (b)	74cm	76cm	79cm	81cm	83cm	85cm	88cm
Yarn amount	765m	825m	900m	955m	1015m	1065m	1140m

Designed to be worn with 5cm positive ease.

materials:

* 8 (9, 9, 10, 11, 11, 12) x 50g balls of Rico Essentials Merino (100 per cent wool), Grey
* 6mm Tunisian hook
* 6 stitch markers
* 3 coat-style toggles

yarn review:

This DK-weight superwash wool is luxuriously soft and hard-wearing.

yarn alternative:

Artesano Superwash

tension:

Work 16 sts and 18 rows in Tunisian knit stitch to measure 10cm square using 6mm hook, or size needed to achieve tension.

special stitches:

See Techniques, page 18 for Tunisian simple stitch (tss), Standard return pass (srp) and Tunisian knit stitch (tks).

Tunisian Knit Stitch 2 Together (tks2tog)
Insert the hook from left to right in each of the next two stitches, YO and pull through all the stitches.

pattern note:

This cardigan is worked from the bottom up, with the shawl collar picked up at the end.

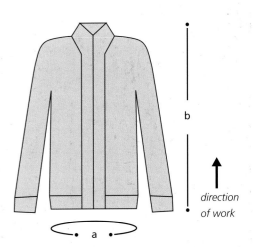

b

a

direction of work

Tunisian knit stitch is one of the basic Tunisian stitches, creating a very warm, thick fabric.

instructions:

Sleeves (Make 2)

Cuff

Make 31 (33, 35, 36, 38, 39, 41)ch.

Row 1: Starting in 2nd ch from hook, 30 (32, 34, 35, 37, 38, 40)tss, srp.

Row 2: 30 (32, 34, 35, 37, 38, 40)tss, srp.

Work row 2 until the cuff measures 5cm.

Sleeve

Row 1: 1tks, 2tks in next, tks to 2sts from end, 2tks in next, 1tks, srp. 32 (34, 36, 37, 39, 40, 42) sts.

Rows 2–5: Tks across, srp.

Work rows 1–5 a total of 10 (10, 11, 11, 12, 12, 13) times. 50 (52, 56, 57, 61, 62, 66) sts.

Work even until the sleeve measures 46 (47,

48, 50, 51, 51, 52) cm from the cuff.

Seam the sleeve up the sides. Place the stitch marker 5 (6, 7, 8, 9, 20, 11) stitches away from the seam on both sides. 11 (13, 15, 17, 19, 21, 23) sts between markers (seam counts as 1 stitch).

Body

Bottom Edging

Make 135 (143, 151, 159, 167, 175, 183)ch.

Row 1: Starting in 2nd ch from hook, 134 (142, 150, 158, 166, 174, 182)tss, srp.

Row 2: 134 (142, 150, 158, 166, 174, 182) tss, srp.

Work row 2 until the edging measures 5cm.

Body

Row 1: 134 (142, 150, 158, 166, 174, 182) tks, srp.

Work row 1 until the piece measures 52 (53, 55, 56, 56, 57, 58)cm.

Join Sleeves

Row 1: 24 (25, 26, 27, 28, 29, 30)tks, pick up sleeve and 39 (39, 41, 40, 42, 41, 43)tks of sleeve, leaving marked armhole sts, miss 11 (13, 15, 17, 19, 21, 23) sts of body, work 64 (66, 68, 70, 72, 74, 76)tks across the back, pick up 2nd sleeve, 39 (39, 41, 40, 42, 41, 43)tks of sleeve, leaving marked armhole sts, miss 11 (13, 15, 17, 19, 21, 23) sts of body, 24 (25, 26, 27, 28, 29, 30)tks, srp. 190 (194, 202, 204, 212, 214, 222) sts.

Work even for 8 rows.

Decreases:

Set-up row: 24 (25, 26, 27, 28, 29, 30)tks,

pm in next, 37 (37, 39, 38, 40, 39, 41)tks, pm in next, 64 (66, 68, 70, 72, 74, 76)tks across the back, pm in next, 37 (37, 39, 38, 40, 39, 41)tks of sleeve, pm in next, 24 (25, 26, 27, 28, 29, 30)tks, srp. 190 (194, 202, 204, 212, 214, 222) sts.

Row 1: [Tks to 2 sts before pm, 1tks2tog, 1tks, 1tks2tog] four times, tks to end, srp. 182 (186, 194, 196, 204, 206, 214) sts.

Row 2: Tks across, srp.

Work rows 1–2 a total of 18 (18, 19, 19, 20, 19, 20) times, 38 (42, 44, 46, 48, 56, 58) sts.

Row 3: Tks all the way across, srp, working

all sts and removing markers.

Row 4: Tks across, srp. Break yarn.

Collar

Rejoin the yarn at the bottom front of the cardigan. Pick up a loop from each row end up the front, from each stitch around the neck and from each row end down the other side of the front, srp. 236 (242, 252, 256, 262, 268, 276) sts.

Rows 1–8: Tss across, srp. Break yarn and weave in the ends.

Finishing

Sew up the opening at the underarms. For toggle loops, 30ch. Using the photos for placement, sew toggles onto the front of the cardigan.

For little ones

****

granny pixie hat

Using a traditional granny stripe pattern and a muted palette gives
this baby hat a lovely vintage feel.

skill level **beginner**

Size	Newborn	Baby	Toddler	Child
Finished hat height	25cm	32cm	36cm	38cm
Finished hat depth	32cm	41cm	43cm	47cm
Yarn amount	100m	120m	150m	200m

materials:

* Colour A: 1 x 25g ball from Mini Cakes Yarn Pack of Libby Summers Fine Aran (50 per cent wool, 50 per cent alpaca), Larama

* Colour B: 1 x 25g ball from Mini Cakes Yarn Pack of Libby Summers Fine Aran (50 per cent wool, 50 per cent alpaca), Pante

* Colour C: 1 x 25g ball from Mini Cakes Yarn Pack of Libby Summers Fine Aran (50 per cent wool, 50 per cent alpaca), Verde

* Colour D: 1 x 25g ball from Mini Cakes Yarn Pack of Libby Summers Fine Aran (50 per cent wool, 50 per cent alpaca), Lima

* Colour E: 1 x 25g ball from Mini Cakes Yarn Pack of Libby Summers Fine Aran (50 per cent wool, 50 per cent alpaca), Kulli

* Colour F: 1 x 25g ball from Mini Cakes Yarn Pack of Libby Summers Fine Aran (50 per cent wool, 50 per cent alpaca), Azule

* 4mm hook

yarn review:

This luscious wool and alpaca blend yarn is soft and perfect for wearing next to the skin.

yarn alternative:

King Cole Merino Blend Aran

tension:

Work 5 clusters and 9 rows in pattern to measure 10cm square using 4mm hook, or size needed to achieve tension.

special stitch:

Granny Stripe

For swatching, chain 21 and follow instructions for rows 1–3. Then work rows 2–3 a total of four times.

pattern notes:

Count the turning chain as a stitch. Change colours at the start of each row, alternating colours A–F as you work each row.

Even in larger sizes, this hat works up quickly and easily for last-minute gift giving.

instructions:

With Colour A, 45 (54, 60, 63)ch.

Row 1: Starting in 6th ch from hook (counts as 1tr and 1ch), [3tr in ch, 1ch, miss 2ch] 13 (16, 18, 19) times, 1tr. Turn. Break yarn. 13 (16, 18, 19) 3tr clusters.

Row 2: Attach new colour, 3ch, 2tr in chsp, [1ch, miss 3tr, 3tr in chsp] 12 (15, 17, 18) times, 2tr in chsp, 1tr in top of tch. Turn. Break yarn. 14 (17, 19, 20) 3tr clusters.

Row 3: Attach new colour, 5ch, miss 3tr, [3tr in chsp, 1ch, miss 3tr] 13 (16, 18, 19) times, 1tr. Turn. Break yarn. 13 (16, 18, 19) 3tr clusters.

Work rows 2–3 a total of 7 (9, 9, 10) times. For sizes toddler and child, work row 2 once more.

Fold the beginning chain in half widthwise and sew or slip stitch the seam closed.

Bottom edging

Row 1: With Colour A, make 10 (11, 12, 13) ch, attach to front bottom edge of hat. Dc around bottom of hat 1dc into each tch and/ or tr around, 11 (12, 13, 14)ch. Turn. 28 (36, 38, 42) sts.

Row 2: Starting in 2nd ch from hook, 48 (58, 62, 68)dc across ch and dc. Break yarn.

Pom-poms (Make 2)

Cut a 30cm piece of contrast yarn and set it aside.

Using the yarn still attached to the ball, secure the cut end of yarn between two of your fingers, take your contrast yarn and wrap it approximately 60 times around your non-dominant hand.

Carefully remove the yarn from your fingers. Pick up the set-aside yarn and wrap it widthwise around the loops of yarn. Tie it off tightly.

Cut the loops, being careful not to cut the securing tie. Fluff up the yarn and trim into a pom-pom shape.

Sew securely to each end of the ties on the hat.

Note: Pom-poms can come undone and present a choking hazard with loose strands of yarn. Children under three years old should not be left unattended with pompoms. If in doubt, leave them off.

pom-pom slippers

Inspired by a pair of sewn booties we were given when our son Ellis was a baby, these have become the go-to gift for new babies in our lives.

skill level **advanced beginner**

Size	6–12 months	1–3 years	3–5 years	5–7 years	7–13 years
Finished foot circumference	11.5cm	14cm	15cm	16.5cm	18cm
Finished length	10cm	13cm	15cm	16.5cm	18cm
Yarn amount: main colour	65m	105m	130m	160m	190m
Yarn amount: contrast colour	30m	30m	30m	30m	30m

Designed to be worn with no ease.

materials:

* Main Colour (MC): 1 x 50g ball of Brown Sheep Nature Spun Sport (100 per cent wool), Charcoal
* Contrast Colour (CC): 1 x 50g ball of Brown Sheep Nature Spun Sport (100 per cent wool), Flamingo (also pictured in Turquoise Wonder)
* 3.75mm hook
* Sew-on snaps
* Stitch marker
* Safety pins

yarn review:

This high-twist 100 per cent wool yarn is hardwearing – perfect for busy feet. It also comes in an astounding array of colours, so you will be able to choose your palette.

yarn alternative:

Rowan Felted Tweed 4 ply

tension:

Work 22 sts and 24 rows in double crochet to measure 10cm square using 3.75mm hook, or size needed to achieve tension.

pattern note:

Do not count turning chains as a stitch.

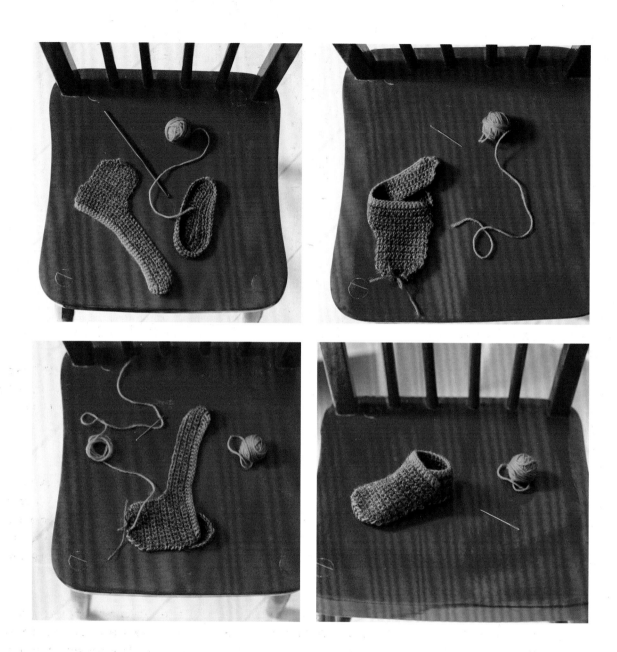

Add a bit of puff paint to the soles to make the slippers non-skid for walkers and crawlers.

instructions:

Soles (Make 2)

With MC, 17 (18, 21, 22, 22)ch.

Round 1: Starting in 2nd ch from hook, 2dc in ch, 4 (4, 5, 5, 5)dc, 6 (7, 8, 8, 8)htr, 4 (4, 5, 6, 6)tr, 4tr in last ch, turning work to work down unworked side of beg ch, 4 (4, 5, 6, 6) tr, 6 (7, 8, 8, 8)htr, 4 (4, 5, 5, 5)dc, 2dc in last ch (this already has 2dc worked into it). Join. 36 (38, 44, 46, 46) sts.

Round 2: 1ch, [2dc in dc] twice, 14 (15, 18, 19, 19)dc, [2dc in tr] four times, 14 (15, 18, 19, 19)dc, [2dc in dc] twice. Join. 44 (46, 52, 54, 54) sts.

Round 3: 1ch, 1dc, pm, 2dc in next, 18 (19, 22, 23, 23)dc, 2dc in next, pm, 2dc, 2dc in next, 18 (19, 22, 23, 23)dc, 2dc in next, pm, 1dc. Join. 48 (50, 56, 58, 58) sts.

For sizes 1–3 years, 3–5 years, 5–7 years and 7–13 years ONLY

Round 4: 1dc, 2dc in next, work to 1st from marker, 2dc in next, 2dc, 2dc in next, work to 2 sts from end of round, 2dc in next, 1dc. Join.

Work round 4 a total of – (1, 2, 4, 5) times. Break yarn. – (54, 64, 74, 78) sts.

Left Upper

With CC, 37 (42, 45, 48, 51)ch.

Row 1 (RS): Starting in 2nd ch from hook, 36 (41, 44, 47, 50)dc. Turn.

Switch to MC, work 5 (7, 11, 15, 17) rows as follows: 1ch, 36 (41, 44, 47, 50)dc. Turn.

Work 24 (29, 38, 47, 51) rows as follows: 1ch, 15 (18, 20, 21, 23)dc. Turn. 15 (18, 21, 23) sts.

Next row: 1ch, 1dc2tog, 11 (14, 16, 17, 19) dc, 1dc2tog. Turn. 13 (16, 18, 19, 21) sts.

Next row: 1ch, 1dc2tog, 9 (12, 14, 15, 17) dc, 1dc2tog. Turn. Break yarn. 11 (14, 16, 17, 19) sts.

Right Upper

With CC, 37 (42, 45, 48, 51)ch.

Row 1 (RS): Starting in 2nd ch from hook, 36 (41, 44, 47, 50)dc. Turn.

Switch to MC, work 5 (7, 11, 15, 17) rows as follows: 1ch, 36 (41, 44, 47, 50)dc. Turn. Break yarn.

Next row: Miss 21 (23, 24, 26, 27)dc, rejoin MC, 1ch, 15 (18, 20, 21, 23)dc. Turn. 15 (18, 20, 21, 23) sts.

Work 23 (28, 37, 46, 50) rows as follows: 1ch, 15 (18, 20, 21, 23)dc.

Next row: 1ch, 1dc2tog, 11 (14, 16, 17, 19) dc, 1dc2tog. Turn. 13 (16, 18, 19, 21) sts.

Next row: 1ch, 1dc2tog, 9 (12, 14, 15, 17) dc, 1dc2tog. Turn. Break yarn. 11 (14, 16, 17, 19) sts.

Sewing Up

Line up the toe of the upper to the toe of the sole. Secure with a pin or a piece of string. Using CC, sew the two pieces together using a whipstitch. Sew around the bottom as shown, bringing the long end of the upper around inside the bootie.

Separate the snap and sew one side to the inside of the outer flap that wraps around the ankle and the other side onto the outside of the inner ankle flap. Make two small pom-poms (see Techniques, page 21) and sew on using the photos for placement.

kite bunting

This pattern only needs small amounts of yarn in each colour, so raid your stash to make a colourful and fun bunting.

skill level **beginner**

Size	One size
Finished length of motif	10cm
Finished width of motif	6cm

materials:

* 1 x 50g ball Artesano Superwash (100 per cent wool), Navy (6416)
* 1 x 50g ball Artesano Superwash (100 per cent wool), Sand Yellow (7254)
* 1 x 50g ball Artesano Superwash (100 per cent wool), Grey (SFN41)
* 1 x 50g ball Artesano Superwash (100 per cent wool), Teal (5167)
* small amount of Artesano Superwash (100 percent wool), Cream (SFNIU)
* 4mm hook
* Tapestry needle

yarn review:

This is a fantastic superwash yarn that is a staple in my yarn stash.

yarn alternatives:

Cascade 220
Debbie Bliss Rialto DK

tension:

1 motif measures 10 x 6cm using 4mm hook, or size needed to achieve tension.

pattern note:

Count the chains at the beginning of the round as a stitch.

Hang high over a window to bring a bit of the outside in.

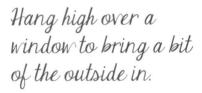

instructions:

Kite (Make 5 to make a 1m length of bunting)

Round 1: Starting with magic loop (see Techniques, page 17), 3ch, 1tr, [2ch, 2tr] three times, 1ch, 2tr, 2ch, 2tr, 1ch. Join with slst into top of 3ch. 6 2tr clusters.

Round 2: Slst to 1st 2chsp, (3ch, 1tr, 2ch, 2tr) into 2chsp, 1ch, [(2tr, 2ch, 2tr) into next 2chsp, 1ch] twice, 2tr into 1chsp, 1ch, (2tr, 2ch, 2tr) into 2chsp, 1ch, 2tr into 1chsp, 1ch. Join with slst into the top of 1st tr. 10 2tr clusters.

Round 3: Slst to 1st 2chsp, (3ch, 1tr, 2ch, 2tr) into 2chsp, [1ch, 2tr into 1chsp, 1ch, (2tr, 2ch, 2tr) into 2chsp] twice, [1ch, 2tr into 1chsp] twice, 1ch, (2tr, 2ch, 2tr) into 2chsp, [1ch, 2tr into 1chsp] twice, 1ch. Join with slst into top of 3ch. 14 2tr clusters.

Round 4: Slst to 1st 2chsp, (3ch, 1tr, 2ch, 2tr) into 2chsp, [(1ch, 2tr) into next 1chsp] twice, [1ch, (2tr, 2ch, 2tr) into 2chsp] twice, [1ch, 2tr in next 1chsp] three times, 1ch, (2tr, 2ch, 2tr) into 2chsp, [1ch, 2tr into next 1chsp] three times, 1ch. Join with slst into top of 1st tr. 18 2tr clusters.

Bows (Make 3 per kite in alternate colours)

Make 6ch.

Row 1: Starting in 2nd stitch from hook, 5dc. Turn. 5dc.

Rows 2–3: 1ch, 5dc. Turn.

Break the yarn, leaving a 10cm tail. Weave the end into the middle of the last row and wrap it tightly around the middle of the piece to make a secure bow.

Tail

Thread three bows onto a 10cm length of yarn, securing each one in place with a knot. Secure the yarn onto the bottom of the motif.

Stringing

With the yarn for string, 10ch, [1dc into top 2chsp of motif, 10dc] five times. 10ch.

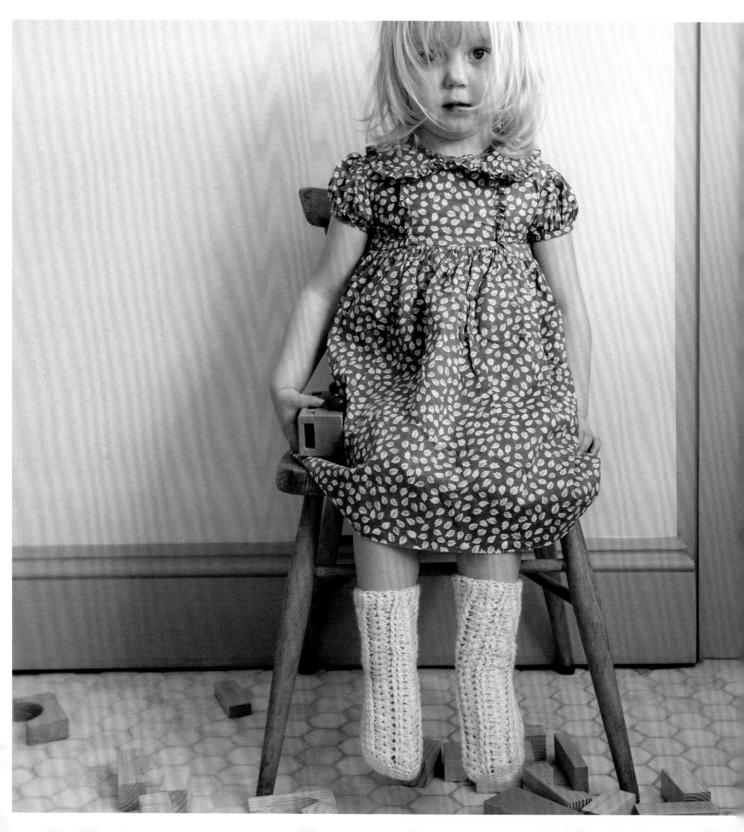

first day of school socks

Send a bit of handmade love with them on their first big
day of school – from nursery to university.

skill level **intermediate**

Size	Baby	Child	Teen	Women's small	Women's large
Finished ankle circumference (a)	12cm	15cm	18cm	21cm	24cm
Finished foot length (b)	10.5cm	15cm	18cm	25cm	28cm
Yarn amount:	180m	220m	290m	400m	540m

Designed to be worn with no ease to 2cm negative ease.

materials:

* 1 (2, 2, 3, 3) x 50g balls of The Fibre Company Canopy (50 per cent alpaca, 30 per cent Merino, 20 per cent Bamboo), Orchid
* 3.75mm hook
* 2 stitch markers
* Tapestry needle

yarn review:

This has to be one of the most gorgeous sock yarns I have ever laid hands on. The bamboo adds sheen and strength to the luxurious softness of the wool and alpaca.

yarn alternative:

Artesano Definition Sock

tension:

Work 20 sts and 20 rows in double crochet to measure 10cm square using 3.75mm hook, or size needed to achieve tension.

special stitches:

Short Row Double Crochet 2 Together (srdc2tog)

Insert the hook into the stitch at the end of the row, YO and pull through, insert hook into the first stitch of the longer row below, YO and pull through. YO, pull through all three loops on the hook. Pull tight to close off any gaps.

Extended Double Crochet (exdc)

Insert the hook into the stitch, YO, pull through, YO, pull through the first loop on the hook, YO, pull through both loops on the hook.

pattern note:

Do not count the turning chain as a stitch.

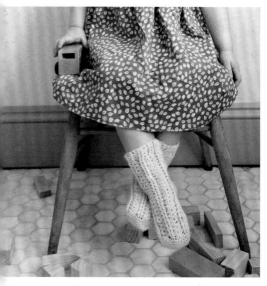

instructions:

Leg Ribbing

Leaving a 10cm tail for sewing up the gap, 20 (25, 30, 35, 40)ftr. Join for working in the round.

Ribbing:

Rounds 1–3 (3, 4, 4, 4): 3ch (does not count as a st), *1RtrB, 1RtrF, 1RtrB, 2RtrF; rep from * around. Join into top of 3ch.

Pattern:

Round 1: 3ch, *miss one, (2tr, 1ch, 2tr) in next, miss one, 2RtrF; rep from * around. Join.

Round 2: 3ch, *miss 2tr, (2tr, 1ch, 2tr) in chsp, miss 2tr, 2RtrF; rep from * around. Join.

Work round 2 until the piece measures 10 (11, 13, 15, 18)cm.

Heel Flap

Row 1 (RS): 2ch (does not count as a st), 2dc, [miss chsp, 6dc] 1 (2, 2, 3, 3) times, 2dc. Turn. 10 (16, 16, 22, 22) sts.

Rows 2–6 (10, 10, 14, 14): 1ch, 10 (16, 16, 22, 22)dc. Turn.

Heel Turn

Row 1 (RS): 1ch, 7 (11, 11, 15, 15)dc. Turn.

Row 2: 1ch, 4 (6, 6, 8, 8)dc. Turn.

Row 3: 1ch, 3 (5, 5, 7, 7), 1srdc2tog. Turn. Rep row 3 until all the stitches in the heel flap row are worked, ending on a RS row. 4 (6, 6, 8, 8) sts.

Foot

Set-up round (RS): 2ch (does not count as a st), 4 (6, 6, 8, 8)exdc, working up sides of heel flap, evenly place 4 (6, 9, 8, 11)exdc,

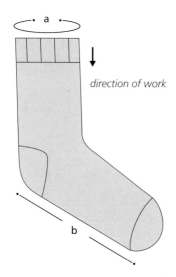

direction of work

2RtrF, [miss 2tr, (2tr, 1ch, 2tr) in chsp, miss 2tr, 2RtrF] 2 (2, 3, 3, 4) times, working down sides of heel flap, evenly place 4 (6, 9, 8, 11)exdc. Join. Do not turn. 26 (32, 44, 44, 56) sts.

Round 1: 2ch, 8 (12, 15, 16, 19)exdc, 2RtrF, [miss 2tr, (2tr, 1ch, 2tr) in chsp, miss 2tr, 2RtrF] 2 (2, 3, 3, 4) times, 4 (6, 9, 8, 11)exdc. Join.

Repeat round 1 until the sock measures 8.5 (13, 14.5, 21.5, 23) cm from the back of the heel.

Toe

This section is worked in the amigurumi style with no joining or raising of the rounds.

Set-up round: 1ch (does not count as a st), 12 (16, 19, 20, 23)dc, [miss next chsp, 6dc] 1 (1, 2, 2, 3) times, 8 (10, 13, 12, 15)dc. Join. 26 (32, 44, 44, 56) sts.

Round 1: 1ch, 13 (16, 22, 22, 28)dc, pm, 13 (16, 22, 22, 28)dc, pm. Join.

Round 2: 1ch, 1dc2tog, work to 2 sts before

marker, 1dc2tog, sm, 1dc2tog, work to 2 sts before end, 1dc2tog. Join.
Repeat round 2 until you have 14 (16, 16, 16, 16)dc remaining.

Making Up
Fold the toe in half and seam the bottom and top together from the inside. Sew up the gap at the cuff. Weave in the ends.

Short row heels can be tricky at first, but don't let them put you off - they have magical properties, turning a flap into a heel neatly and evenly.

breton top

This scrumptious little top is a simple and sweet make.

skill level **intermediate**

Size	6 months	18 months	2 years	4 years	6 years	8 years
Finished chest circumference (a)	44cm	48cm	53cm	59cm	62cm	67cm
Finished length (b)	22cm	25cm	27cm	28cm	29cm	31cm
Yarn amounts (MC)	330m	370m	445m	555m	615m	800m

Designed to be worn with 0–1cm positive ease.

materials:

* Main Colour (MC): 3 (3, 3, 4, 4, 5) x 50g balls of MillaMia (100 per cent wool), Navy
* Contrast Colour (CC): 1 x 50g balls of MillaMia (100 per cent wool), White
* 4mm hook
* Tapestry needle
* 4 (4, 4, 5, 5, 6) x 1cm diameter buttons

yarn review:

This sport-weight wool is washable and light, making it an excellent choice for children's clothes.

yarn alternatives:

Cascade 220 Superwash Sport
Brown Sheep Nature Spun Sport

tension:

Work 16 sts and 11 rows in paired treble crochet to measure 10cm square using 4mm hook, or size needed to achieve tension.

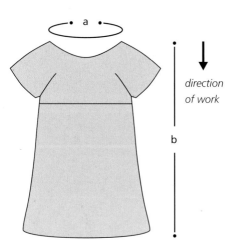

direction of work

special stitches:

Paired Treble Crochet (ptr)

For Swatch:

Make an odd number of chains.

Row 1: 1tr in 3rd ch from hook, 1tr in same chain, *miss 1ch, 2tr into next ch; repeat from * to last 2 sts, miss 1ch, 1tr. Turn.

Row 2: 3ch (counts as 1tr), *2tr in space between 2tr; rep from * across 1tr into top of tch.

Work row 2 until the piece measures at least 10cm from the beginning chain.

Linked Treble Crochet (ltr)

Insert the hook into the middle loop of the stitch just worked, YO, pull the loop through, hook into the next stitch, YO, pull the loop through, YO, pull the loop through two loops on the hook, YO, pull through the last two loops.

Linked Treble Crochet after 3 Chain

Insert the hook into the middle chain, YO, pull the loop through, hook into the next stitch, YO, pull the loop through, YO, pull the loop through two loops on the hook, YO, pull through the last two loops.

pattern notes:

Count the tch as a stitch.

The bodice is designed to be quite fitted. For more ease, go up a size or work an extra repeat of bodice rows 2–3.

instructions:

Bodice

Make 40 (42, 42, 44, 44, 44)ch.

Set-up row (WS): Starting in 4th ch from hook (counts as 1tr), 3ltr, [miss 1tr, 2tr in next] twice, 1tr, [miss 1tr, 2tr in next] twice, 1tr, [miss 1tr, 2tr in next] 5 (6, 6, 7, 7, 7) times, 1tr, [miss 1tr, 2tr in next] twice, 1tr, [miss 1tr, 2tr in next] twice, 4ltr. Turn. 38 (40, 40, 42, 42, 42) sts.

Row 1 (RS): 3ch, 3ltr, miss tr, 2tr in sp btwn 2tr, miss 2tr, 4tr in sp btwn 2tr, miss 1tr, 1RtrF, [miss 1tr, 4tr in sp btwn 2tr, miss 1tr] twice, 1RtrF, miss 1tr, 4tr in sp btwn 2tr, miss 1tr, [miss 1tr, 2tr in sp btwn 2tr, miss 1tr] 3 (4, 4, 5, 5, 5) times, miss 1tr, 4tr in sp btwn 2tr, miss 1tr, 1RtrF, [miss 1tr, 4tr in sp btwn 2tr, miss 1tr] twice, 1RtrF, miss 1tr, 4tr in sp btwn 2tr, miss 2tr, 2tr in sp btwn 2tr, 4ltr. Turn. 54 (56, 56, 58, 58, 58) sts.

Row 2 and all WS rows: 3ch, 3ltr, work ptr into each ptr and 1RtrB into each RtrF across, 4ltr.

Row 3: 3ch, 3ltr, *miss 1tr, 2tr in sp btwn 2tr, miss 1tr; rep from * to 2tr before RtrB, miss 1tr, 4tr in sp btwn 2tr, miss 1tr, RtrF, [miss 1tr, 4tr in sp btwn 2tr, miss 1tr, **miss 1tr, 2tr in sp btwn 2tr, miss 1; rep from ** to 2tr before RtrB, miss 1tr, 4tr in sp btwn 2tr, miss 1, RtrF] three times, ^miss 1tr, 2tr in sp btwn 2tr, miss 1tr; rep from ^ to ltr, 4ltr. Turn. 62 (64, 64, 66, 66, 66) sts.

Work rows 2 and 3 a total of 2 (3, 4, 4, 5, 5) times. 86 (96, 104, 106, 114, 114) sts.

Work even in pattern for 4 (1, 2, 4, 4, 6) rows.

Joining work in the round:

With RS facing, overlap the two sections of ltr, with the left side of the yoke to the front. Working through both layers of fabric, 3ch (does not count as a stitch), 3tr *miss 1tr, 2tr in sp btwn 2tr, miss 1tr; rep from * to RtrF, miss RtrF, 10 (10, 10, 14, 18, 20)ftr, miss RtrF, miss 16 (20, 20, 20, 24, 24)tr, *miss 1tr, 2tr in sp btwn 2tr, miss 1tr; rep from * to RtrF, miss RtrF, 10 (10, 10, 14, 18, 20)ftr, mis RtrF, miss 16 (20, 20, 20, 24, 24)tr, miss next RtrF, *miss 1tr, 2tr in sp btwn 2tr, miss 1tr; rep from * to beginning. Join.

Break the yarn and rejoin under the middle of the right armhole. 74 (76, 84, 94, 102, 106) sts.

Body

Row 1: Using MC, 3ch (counts as 1tr), 2tr in each tr around. Join 148 (152, 168, 188, 204, 212) sts.

Row 2: 3ch, 1tr in each stitch around. Join.

Row 3: Using CC, 1ch (does not count as a st), 1dc in each tr around. Join.

Work rows 1–3 a total of 9 (9, 12, 15, 15, 18) times.

Finishing

Using the beginning chains from the yoke as buttonholes, evenly space your buttons on the edge of the opening and sew securely. Weave in the ends.

Light and floaty, this is a perfect top to wear over jeans – or make the striped section longer for a dress.

granny chevron blanket

Strongly inspired by quilts, granny squares get a seriously modern update with this twist on granny square blankets.

skill level **beginner**

Size	Throw	Single bed	Double bed
Width	90cm	180cm	210cm
Length	90cm	225cm	225cm
Colour A	440m	1870m	2090m
Colour B	440m	1980m	2200m

The photos show throw size.

materials:

* Colour A: 4 (17, 19) x 100g balls of Texere Chunky Wool (100 per cent wool), Slate
* Colour B: 4 (18, 20) x 100g balls of Texere Chunky Wool (100 per cent wool), Mustard
* 5.5mm hook

yarn review:

This chunky wool is 100 per cent British and comes in a range of gorgeous colours.

yarn alternatives:

Artesano British Wool Chunky
Wendy Mode Chunky

tension:

Work one granny square motif to measure 15cm square.

pattern notes:

For each colour change, drop the working colour and pick up the new colour. Leave the dropped colour where it hangs. You will come back to it in the second half of the next round.

Count the 3ch at the beginning of each round as 1tr.

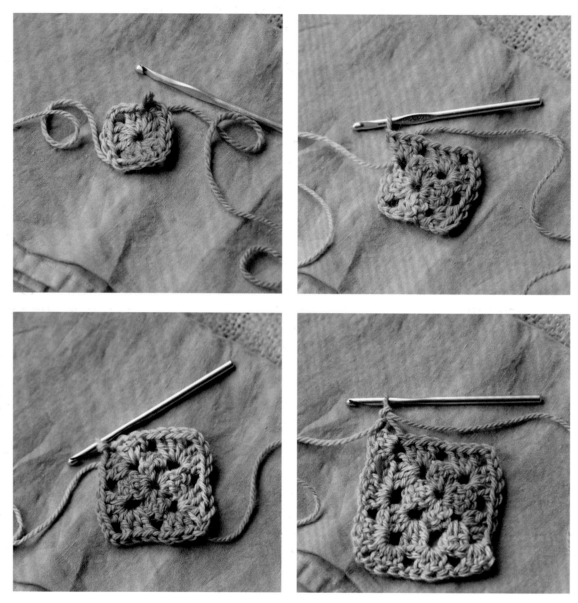

For further layout inspiration, look to quilting resources for Half Square Triangles.

special technique:

Switching colours (switch to)

To give the neatest switch between colours: Leaving one loop of working yarn on the hook, pick up the next colour, 2ch only with the new colour, YO, pull through both the old colour and the new colour loops on the hook.

instructions:

Granny Square (Make 36 (180, 210))

With Colour A, 3ch. Join in the round with a slst.

Round 1: Working into centre of 3ch loop, 3ch (counts as 1tr), 2tr, 2ch, 3tr, 2ch, leaving 1 loop on hook, join Colour B, 2ch and YO, pull through both loops on hook (counts as 1tr), 2tr, 2ch, 3tr, 2ch. Join with slst into top of 3ch. Turn.

Round 2: Continuing with Colour B, slst to centre of 2chsp, (3ch, 2tr) into chsp, 1ch, (3tr, 2ch, 3tr) into next chsp, (3tr, 2ch) into chsp, switch to Colour A, (3ch (counts as 1tr) 2tr) into next chsp, 1ch, (3tr, 2ch, 3tr) into next chsp, 1ch, (3tr, 2ch) into chsp you started the round with. Join into top of 3ch. Turn.

Round 3: Continuing with Colour A, slst to centre of 2chsp, (3ch, 2tr) into chsp, 1ch, 3tr in next chsp, 1ch, (3tr, 2ch, 3tr) in next chsp, 1ch, 3tr in next chsp, 1ch, (3tr, 1ch, switch to Colour B, 1ch, 3tr) in next chsp, 1ch, 3tr in next chsp, 1ch, (3tr, 2ch, 3tr) in next chsp, 1ch, 3tr in next chsp, 1ch, (3tr, 2ch) into chsp you started the round with. Join into top of 3ch. Turn.

Round 4: Continuing with Colour B, slst to centre of 2chsp, (3ch, 2tr) into chsp, [1ch, 3tr in next chsp] twice, 1ch, (3tr, 2ch, 3tr) in next chsp, [1ch, 3tr in next chsp] twice, 1ch, (3tr, 1ch, switch to Colour A, 1ch, 3tr) in next chsp, [1ch, 3tr in next chsp] twice, 1ch, (3tr, 2ch, 3tr) in next chsp, [1ch, 3tr in next chsp] twice, 1ch, (3tr, 2ch) into chsp you started the round with. Join into top of 3ch.

Assembling

Using the illustrations as a guide, align the squares in pattern.

* The throw is laid out six squares wide by six squares tall.
* The single blanket is laid out 12 squares wide by 15 squares tall.
* The double blanket is laid out 14 squares wide by 15 squares tall.

Join the granny squares in vertical rows. Place two squares RS together. Starting in one corner, working through both sets of stitches, dc into each tr and chsp across until you come to the next corner. Pick up another two squares, hold them RS together and continue working in the same way until all of the stitches are worked. Work in this manner until the entire first row is joined.

Work the following rows by aligning one square to the opposite side of the already joined squares. Continue in this manner until all of the vertical rows are worked.

Join the horizontal rows by aligning adjacent squares and dc into each tr and chsp across.

single bed

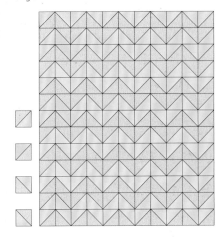

throw

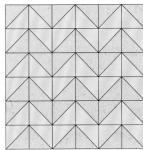

Edging

Round 1: Join Colour B to corner of blanket, 1ch, work 1dc into each tr and chsp around. Work (2dc, 3ch, 2dc) into each of four corners of joined blanket. Join into 1st dc with slst.

Round 2: 1dc in each dc around. Work (2dc, 3ch, 2dc) into each of four corners of joined blanket. Join into 1st dc with slst.

lacy yoke cardigan

Sweet lace at the collar creates impact on this a pretty little make.

skill level **intermediate**

Size	Newborn	Baby	1–2 years	2 years	4 years	6 years	8 years	10 years
To fit chest (a)	42cm	45cm	48cm	53cm	58cm	64cm	68cm	72cm
Length (b)	21cm	23cm	25cm	28cm	30cm	33cm	38cm	42cm
Main colour	175m	205m	240m	290m	350m	415m	515m	595m
Contrast colour	86m	105m	120m	145m	175m	205m	255m	300m

Cardigan is sized to be worn with 5cm positive ease.

materials:

* Colour A: 2 (2, 3, 3, 4, 4, 5, 6) 50g balls of Artesano Superwash DK (100 per cent wool), Sand Yellow
* Colour B: 1 (1, 1, 2, 2, 2, 3, 3) 50g balls of Artesano Superwash DK (100 per cent wool), Grey
* 5mm hook
* 8 (9, 10, 10, 11, 12, 15, 16) buttons 1cm in diameter
* 5 stitch markers

tension:

Work 8 sts and 4.5 rows in linked treble to measure 10cm square using 5mm hook, or size needed to achieve tension.

special stitches:

Linked Treble Crochet (ltr)

Insert the hook into the middle loop of the stitch just worked, YO, pull the loop through, hook into the next stitch, YO, pull the loop through, YO, pull the loop through two loops on the hook, YO, pull through the last two loops.

Linked Treble Crochet after 3 Chain

Insert the hook into the middle chain, YO, pull the loop through, hook into the next stitch, YO, pull the loop through, YO, pull the loop through two loops on the hook, YO, pull through the last two loops.

For a more subtle design, make the cardigan all in one colour.

pattern note:

Count the tch at the beginning of each row as a stitch.

instructions:

Lace Collar and Yoke

With Colour A, make 55 (60, 60, 65, 65, 65, 70, 70)ch.

Row 1 (WS): Starting in 2nd ch from hook, 54 (59, 59, 64, 64, 64, 69, 69)dc. Turn.

Row 2: 3ch, 1tr, [miss 2dc, (2tr, 2ch, 2tr) in next, miss 2dc] 10 (11, 11, 12, 12, 12, 13, 13) times, 2tr. Turn. 44 (48, 48, 52, 52, 52, 56, 56) sts.

Rows 3–4: 3ch, 1tr, [miss 2tr, (3tr, 2ch, 3tr) in 2chsp, miss 2tr] 10 (11, 11, 12, 12, 12, 13, 13) times, 2tr. Turn. 64 (70, 70, 76, 76, 76, 82, 82) sts.

Row 5: 3ch, 1tr, [miss 3tr, (4tr, 2ch, 4tr) in 2chsp, miss 3tr] 10 (11, 11, 12, 12, 12, 13, 13) times, 2tr. Turn. 84 (92, 92, 100, 100, 100, 108, 108) sts.

For sizes Newborn and Baby ONLY

Row 6: 3ch, 1tr, [miss 4tr, 8tr in 2chsp, miss 4tr] 10 (11, -, -, -, -, -, -) times, 2tr. Turn. 84 (92, -, -, -, -, -, -)sts.

For 1-2y, 2y, 4y, 8, 10y sizes ONLY

Row 6: 3ch, [miss 4tr, (4tr, 2ch, 4tr) in 2chsp, miss 4tr] - (11,11,12,12,12,13,13) times, 2tr. Turn.

Row 7: 3ch, 1tr, [miss 4tr, (5tr, 2ch, 5tr) in 2chsp, miss 4tr] - (-, 11, 12, 12, 12, 13, 13) times, 2tr. Turn. - (-, 114, 124, 124, 124, 134, 134) sts.

Row 8: 3ch, 1tr, [miss 5tr, (10tr) in 2chsp,

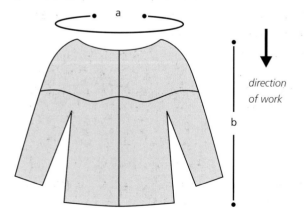

a

direction of work

b

miss 5tr] - (-, 11, 12, 12, 12, 13, 13) times, 2tr. Turn. - (-, 114, 124, 124, 124, 134, 134) sts.

Body

For ALL sizes

Row 1: With RS facing, join Colour B, working in BLO, 3ch, ltr in each stitch across, inc 2 (5, 0, 0, 0, 4, 0, 3) times evenly spaced across row. Turn. 86 (97, 114, 124, 124, 128, 134, 137) sts.
Work even in ltr for 1 (1, 0, 0, 2, 3, 4, 5) rows.

Divide for Armholes

Row 1: 3ch, 13 (14, 16, 17, 18, 20, 21, 22) ltr, 9 (9, 7, 9, 11, 12, 14, 15)ch, miss 14 (17, 21, 24, 22, 21, 22, 22)tr, 1tr, 29 (32, 37, 39, 41, 43, 45, 47)ltr, 9 (9, 7, 9, 11, 12, 14, 15) ch, miss 14 (17, 21, 24, 22, 21, 22, 22)tr, 1tr,

13 (14, 16, 17, 18, 20, 21, 22)ltr. Turn. 58 (63, 72, 76, 80, 86, 90, 93) sts.
Work even in ltr (working into both chains and stitches for first row) for 10 (11, 12, 13, 13, 14, 18, 20) rows. 76 (81, 86, 94, 102, 110, 118, 123) sts. Break yarn.

Sleeves (Make 2)

Round 1: Rejoin Colour B at centre of underarm sts, RS facing. Working into other side of ch and each st around, 3ch, 22 (25, 27, 32, 32, 32, 35, 36)ltr. Join into top of tch. Turn. 23 (26, 28, 33, 33, 33, 36, 37) sts. Work even in ltr for 10 (12, 14, 17, 20, 23, 26, 27) rows. Break yarn.

Button Band

Row 1: Rejoin Colour A in bottom front hem, RS facing. Make 2dc into end of each

row to collar. Turn. 38 (40, 44, 46, 50, 54, 64, 70) sts.

Rows 2–3: 1ch, dc across. Turn.

Buttonholes (work on right front facing side for girls)

Row 1: Rejoin Colour A in bottom front hem, WS facing. Make 2dc into end of each row to collar. Turn. 38 (40, 44, 46, 50, 54, 64, 70) sts.

Row 2: 1ch, dc across. Turn.

Row 3: 1ch, [3dc, 1ch, miss 1dc] 9 (9, 10, 11, 12, 13, 15, 17) times, 2 (4, 4, 2, 2, 2, 4, 2)dc. Break yarn. 29 (31, 34, 35, 38, 41, 49, 53) sts.

Finishing

Using the buttonholes as a guide, sew on your buttons.

Sources for Supplies

To find a local source for the yarns used in this book, contact the manufacturers below.

Artesano Ltd
Makers of alpaca and merino wools.
http://www.artesanoyarns.co.uk/

Cascade Yarns
Manufacturers of a wide range of wools.
http://www.cascadeyarns.com

Coats and Crafts
Suppliers of Patons yarns.
http://www.coatscrafts.co.uk/Products/Knitting/

Designer Yarns
Providers of Debbie Bliss wools.
http://www.designeryarns.uk.com/

Eden Cottage Yarns
Hand-dyed wool from Yorkshire.
http://www.edencottageyarns.co.uk/

Erika Knight Wools
British wools in gorgeous muted pallets.
http://www.erikaknight.co.uk/

Fireside Yarn
Supplier of recycled cotton jersey yarn.
http://www.firesideyarn.co.uk/

Fyberspates
Hand-dyed yarn in a range of weights and fibres.
http://www.fyberspates.co.uk/

Jamieson's
Suppliers of Shetland wool.
http://www.jamiesonsofshetland.co.uk/

Libby Summers Ltd
Purveyor of Peruvian wool and alpaca yarns.
http://www.libbysummers.co.uk/

Malabrigo Yarns
Providers of a range of wool in beautiful hand-dyed colours.
http://www.malabrigoyarn.com/

Magpielly Yarns
Selling Brown Sheep Yarns.
http://www.magpielly.co.uk

MillaMia
Manufacturers of DK-weight superwash merino.
http://www.millamia.com/

Nutscene 1922
Makers of garden twine.
http://www.nutscene.com/

Quince and Co.
Gorgeous yarns in a range of subtle colours and variety of weights.
http://quinceandco.com/

Ripples Crafts
Beautiful hand-dyed yarn, inspired by the landscape of Assynt.
https://www.ripplescrafts.com/

Rico Design
A range of beautiful and affordable cotton and wool yarns.
http://www.rico-design.de/

Rowan Yarns
Providers of a huge range of yarns in most weights and fibres.
http://www.knitrowan.com/

Sublime Yarns/Sirdar Spinning Ltd
Manufacturers of Sublime and Sirdar yarns.
http://www.sirdar.co.uk/home

Other Craft Supplies
Yarns, Hooks and Other Notions

UK
Loop Knitting
http://www.loopknittingshop.com

McA Direct
http://www.mcadirect.com

Australia
Morris and Sons
http://morrisandsons.com.au/

The Wool Shack
http://www.thewoolshack.com/

New Zealand
Knit World
http://www.knitting.co.nz/

The Yarn Studio
http://www.theyarnstudio.co.nz/

Wooden and Branch Buttons:
Little Woodlanders
http://www.etsy.com/shop/LittleWoodlanders

Index

Acknowledgements

To my truly amazing friend, tech editor, support and partner in all things crochet, Joanne Scrace – thank you doesn't really cover how much I appreciate everything you do.

Thanks to the truly dream team of Vicky Orchard (editor), Nadine Tubbs (stylist) and Louise Leffler (designer) for bringing my work to life with such artistry. Kyle Books makes the most beautiful books and I am honoured to have mine amongst them. Thank you as well to Abbi Rose Crook for her make-up artistry, our collection of models – Sinead, Chelsea, Steve, Alberto, Lara, Iris and Greta, and to Boden for supplying their wardrobes. Thanks as always to Clare Hulton, agent extraordinaire, for all her hard work behind the scenes. Thank you to my sample makers – Joanne, Rita, Jacqui, Elly and Jessica. I couldn't have done it without you!

Thanks to my long-suffering business partner, Kat Molesworth, for unending advice and for taking the reins when I have to hide away to write books.

Thank you to my friends and family: Julia, Kerstin, David and Ingrid for jumping in to help whenever and wherever it's needed as we try to juggle book and house, business and life – even if it's just a bottle of wine or a slice of cake at exactly the right moment.

And finally, thank you to Kevin, Ellis, Theo and Georgia – I love you more than anything.